"This Isn't Quite What I Had in Mind"

A Career Planning Program for College Students

by

John W. Loughary, Ph.D.
and
Theresa M. Ripley, Ph.D.

Revised Edition
including a new section on leisure activities
and updated career information.

FOLLETT PUBLISHING COMPANY
Chicago

Library of Congress Cataloging in Publication Data

Loughary, John William, 1930–
This isn't quite what I had in mind.

Bibliography: p.
1. Vocational guidance. I. Ripley, Theresa M., joint author. II. Title.
HF5381.L67 1978 331.7'02 77-27581
ISBN 0-695-80921-0

Contents

This program contains career development materials for college and community college students. Used individually, the program requires from 20-25 hours to complete. The material can also be used as the basis for seminars, workshops and career development classes.

CAREERS
1

USING THE PROGRAM

The fact that you are reading this suggests that you have some concerns about your future.

One purpose of the academic preparation you are completing is to prepare you to survive in and enjoy living in a larger world. During the process of gaining an education you may have acquired fairly specific professional skills. Or you may be at the other end of the continuum, having gained a liberal education with little to offer an employer. Or at least, many sense that to be true.

Whatever the nature of your college study, there are bound to be obstacles in the path of making the transition from school to career. This program is designed to assist you to make a smooth, effective and rewarding transition.

Career development by our definition is a process that never ends. It continues throughout life. Effective career development, like a number of other things, requires a specific set of skills, a knowledge of certain concepts, and accurate information. More specifically, to be an effective career planner you need skills, concepts, and information in the following five aspects of career development:

1. First, you need an up-to-date understanding of yourself. What are your current interests, values, aptitudes, and abilities?
2. You should have a general understanding of the world of work. There are approximately 40,000 job titles at last count, and you must know how to focus on those that are appealing to you. It is also helpful to have some understanding of the many non-occupational activities which can add to career satisfaction.
3. Career payoffs and life style is the third aspect of career development. What is it that turns you on? Is it money, status, influence, or the opportunity to make a difference? How will your occupation affect your total life style? It is important for you to know your personal payoff system so you can seek an environment where relevant opportunities exist.
4. Making effective decisions is a concern faced by all of us as we approach the termination of college. There often seems to be a "decision overload." There are decisions about post-college activities, personal relationships, and a number of other concerns. Decision-making can be done rationally in a series of fairly well-defined steps, and at the same time be responsive to humanistic concerns.
5. The fifth aspect is concerned with implementing decisions. Sometimes a person makes a great decision, but then takes no steps to implement it either because they lack the skills or the motivation or both. There are specific means you can use to overcome this difficulty.

Most students, we find, are not taught the career planning skills, concepts, and information in any of their academic classes during college. Thus, it is understandable that you approach career decisions with a certain amount of trepidation, confusion, and frustration. This program has been designed to assist you in the career decision-making process. The career planning skills can help to alleviate some of the confusion and frustration and assist you to move from college to a satisfying post-college situation.

The materials in this program can be used individually, with a partner, or in a group. If the materials are used in a group, such as a course or a workshop, your group leader will specify instructions for using the materials. The advantages of the group situation are the possibility of dialogue with other people and the presence of a group leader to keep things moving.

To use the program individually, read this section first. Then scan each of the remaining sections and complete those which appeal to you. If you have no particular priorities, we recommend doing the sections in the order presented. In any case, do complete the data sheets and reflect upon the information you generate. Make notes, raise questions, and follow through with any plans and ideas which occur to you. One advantage of the individual approach is that you can complete the exercises according to your own time schedule. A second advantage is the opportunity to be completely open in doing the exercises, since you do not have to share your responses with anyone. But, remember, part of the value of the experience is the possibility to discuss and clarify your replies with another person. Make your own decision on this point. The individual method is generally the most difficult because you are strictly dependent upon yourself.

Completing the program with a partner is an interesting and profitable way to use the materials. Choose someone with whom you would like to share fairly personal experiences and opinions, and who is also a good listener and clarifier. If you decide to do the program with a partner, first read this section and then decide together which of the remaining sections you would like to do. Complete the data sheets independently and then the suggested questions. Try to establish a procedure in which each of you listens to the other. Be sure that (1) you listen and react to their concerns, and (2) they listen and react to yours. It's an "it takes two to tango" sort of thing.

THE MEANING OF CAREER

We are going to be concerned about career planning as we complete the various exercises in this program, so let's establish a common understanding of the meaning of **Career**. Historically, a career was defined more or less as how people earned a living. Thus career was synonymous with "occupation" — or job. A career was being a banker, nurse, teacher, clerk, factory worker, secretary, or housewife, for example. The traditional definition of career as occupation is in large part a reflection of economic conditions. In times past, the work day and week consumed a major part of people's lives, and most of the remaining hours were needed for self and family maintenance.

These circumstances are now changing for an increasing number of people. The work week is shorter, many jobs are less demanding, an increasing number of people are over-educated for the jobs available to them, and self and family maintenance are no longer as time consuming. In short, for an increasing number of people, career means more than occupation or job. In the 1970's we can define career as those major activities which are of prime importance during people's lives. Further, we can specify three criteria for identifying these major activities: (1) they meet basic survival needs, (2) they contribute to a sense of self-fulfillment, or (3) they bring pleasure and happiness. We have labeled each of these activities as follows:

JOB—What you do to survive.

VOCATION—Your most important activities — whatever turns you on.

LEISURE—What you do for fun and relaxation.

For some people one activity can meet all three criteria. For example, the activity "teaching" provides an income, most likely provides a sense of self-fulfillment, and may even at times be fun to do. On the other hand, driving a gravel truck may serve only to provide an income. The truck driver may do leather craft as a means of achieving self-fulfillment, and turn to bowling as a chief leisure activity. Even though the specific nature of a career differs with each individual, a career is often more than an occupation. A career consists of those major activities which are of prime importance during one's life.

The definitions just given for job and leisure are pretty obvious. But you may be somewhat puzzled over our definition of "vocation"—namely, "those activities which provide a sense of self-fulfillment." You may have thought, "Why not use the term avocation?" That is a reasonable question and there is a good answer. Our intent is to emphasize the idea that the most satisfying activities in your life—your vocation, if you will—can have little or nothing to do with how you earn a living. Given the relative affluence which surrounds us on the one hand, and the boredom inherent in many jobs on the other, more people will turn to non-job activities to gain a sense of worth, of contribution, of meaning, of self-fulfillment. Such activities, furthermore, should not be viewed as "extra"; that is, as avocational. Given an adequate income, such activities are of prime importance: they are for many—vocation.

The practical importance of the distinction between job and vocation is to separate job seeking and vocational planning as two often related, but different tasks. Each has its own objectives. When your job must also be the chief source of self-fulfillment, or when your vocation must also provide an income, needless constraints may be imposed.

The following exercise is designed to let you apply this concept of career to your current situation.

In the first column below list activities in which you have participated in the last year. Then check (√) in the columns whether you define the activity as a job, vocation, or leisure activity or some combination of the three. That is, one activity could have 1, 2, or 3 checkmarks.

ACTIVITY	I define this activity as a:		
	Job	Vocation	Leisure

After you have listed several activities, project what would be a satisfying life style for you 2-4 years in the future. In other words, note below what would be for you a perfect mix of: job, vocation, leisure.

What can you do between now and then to achieve this life style?

SELF-UNDERSTANDING
2

Increasing self-understanding is a goal of many college students. The term self-understanding has different meanings for different people and includes many intellectual, psychological and physical aspects of self. In this section we have limited our concern to six areas of self-understanding. Completing the activities that follow can assist you to develop a clearer perspective of some areas of self which can provide a useful basis for career planning. The areas are:

VALUES—your opinions and attitudes

ABILITIES—your skills based on past experience

INTERESTS—your likes and dislikes as related to career activities

SOCIAL ISSUES—the effect of local, national, and international issues on your behavior

IMPORTANT OTHERS—the impact influential others have on your self perception and decision making

FEELING STATES—your ability to identify and describe your own feelings.

This section has one exercise devoted to each aspect of self-understanding. There is no prescribed order in which they should be completed.

VALUES

- *The purpose of this exercise is to increase understanding of your current value structure and contrast it with that of three years ago.*

College students often experience a change in values. This is understandable. Prior to going to college, most students are closely affected by the values of their family and home community. College brings greater freedom and a wider diversity of experiences. This makes an ideal climate for the examination and subsequent change in values.

This exercise is concerned with understanding and describing your values. It is not concerned with judging those values. From our point of view, it is seldom possible to label a value as good or bad; but it is possible to estimate the extent to which other people agree with our values.

One other point about values. Many times two or more values held by a person will conflict. For example, suppose a college sophomore discovers that she's pregnant and that her values do not exclude having an abortion. This girl also places a high value on meeting the expectations of her parents. Her parents are violently opposed to abortion. Thus two values are in conflict and her decision must take into consideration the two conflicting values. Many career decisions involve value conflicts. Resolving value conflicts, both between others and yourself, is easier if you can clearly describe each of the values that are concerned.

VALUES INVENTORY

In the following exercise five value areas have been chosen for examination. After reading each definition, use the spaces provided to describe the current values you hold in that area and the values you held in that area three years ago.

Social and Moral Values: Consider your current and historical reactions to such issues as abortion, premarital sex, marriage, racial and sexual prejudice and discrimination, ecological concerns, and urban vs. rural living. List those moral and social concerns that have been of particular importance in your thinking and development.

CURRENT VALUES

VALUES THREE YEARS AGO

Political Values: Recent national and international political events have caused many people to examine their political opinions and attitudes. Describe both your past and current political orientation; if there has been a change, note events which caused the change.

CURRENT VALUES

VALUES THREE YEARS AGO

Religious Values: Some students find "religion" when they come to college and others lose it. Religious beliefs are a common topic among students. Summarize your thinking about personal beliefs and concerns regarding religion, and list them for the two time periods.

CURRENT VALUES

VALUES THREE YEARS AGO

Economic/Material Values: If you can live without your stereo, you are "into" non-materialism! Describe your current concept of "the good life." Then contrast it with your values three years ago. Compare the material goods valued in each period.

CURRENT VALUES

VALUES THREE YEARS AGO

Aesthetic Values: What do you find aesthetically pleasing today vs. three years ago (e.g., art/painting, film, nature, jewelry, athletics). Describe the importance of aesthetic things in your life today and three years ago.

CURRENT VALUES

VALUES THREE YEARS AGO

Review and share the contents of the Data Sheet. Specifically, think about and discuss the following:

- Rank order the five value areas in order of importance to you, both as of now and as of three years ago and compare the two rankings.
- If you have had some changes in values, what caused the changes?
- Discuss whether you believe you will change any of your values significantly in the next five years. Why or why not?
- What impact do your values have on your career planning?

ABILITIES

- *The purpose of this exercise is to assist you to use past experiences as a basis for describing your abilities.*

One of the first tasks in career planning is to do a self-analysis with particular emphasis on the skills and abilities that can be offered to a potential employer. Many college students have never tried to do a self-analysis of this kind. A thorough self-analysis goes beyond listing technical skills and includes consideration of personal skills and attributes you can bring to a job.

Students often attempt to describe abilities by listing courses they have completed. That is, they often list experiences, when it would be more informative to describe the abilities resulting from those experiences. Another common mistake made by students is not translating the skills they have used to complete college into those needed in the job environment. For example, if you have completed several years of college, you must have developed some organization and planning skills. These skills are also needed in a work environment.

Consider, for example, two recent graduates in sociology whose course work was similar. Both are applying to a computer manufacturer for a sales management trainee position and have been asked to write a paragraph describing their abilities.

Robin Smith: I majored in sociology, with special emphasis in small group procedures. I also completed work in organizational development and statistics. During my senior year I did volunteer tutoring in public schools. I like to work with people and enjoy a wide variety of recreational activities.

Terry Brown: My sociology major helped develop several competencies which should be useful in a sales management position. I have developed skills for helping small groups to define their objectives and work effectively toward them. I have had an opportunity to practice organizational skills in a laboratory or simulation setting and am eager to develop these further in the "real world." I have also had an opportunity to apply research and statistical skills in both process and outcome field studies. Serving as a public school volunteer during my senior year provided a valuable opportunity to use these competencies to "sell" education to students who were very discouraged regarding school. I find that my wide recreational interests provide an effective basis for relating to people with a variety of backgrounds.

The point is simple, but often overlooked by recent or soon-to-be graduates in search of positions. Employers are generally more interested in what applicants can do—rather than the courses they have completed.

This exercise provides practice in conceptualizing and describing experiences—both personal and academic—in terms of the abilities and skills involved. There are two parts to the exercise. The first part is an inventory of your past experiences, and in the second part you are encouraged to analyze your current abilities.

ABILITY INVENTORY

Part I. List five successful and five unsuccessful experiences in each area.

PAID & NON-PAID WORK	ACADEMIC	EXTRA-CURRICULAR	HUMAN RELATIONSHIPS
Successful	Successful	Successful	Successful
1.	1.	1.	1.
2.	2.	2.	2.
3.	3.	3.	3.
4.	4.	4.	4.
5.	5.	5.	5.
Unsuccessful	Unsuccessful	Unsuccessful	Unsuccessful
1.	1.	1.	1.
2.	2.	2.	2.
3.	3.	3.	3.
4.	4.	4.	4.
5.	5.	5.	5.

Share Part I of the inventory and give a brief description of each experience listed. Discuss what made the experience successful or unsuccessful. Focus the discussion on the skills and abilities that were utilized in each experience, and how these abilities and skills affected the success or non-success of the experience. Utilizing the information from Part I, complete Part II of the inventory.

Part II

Each space in Column 1 notes a different kind of ability. Beginning with the first skill (managing/organizing) note in Column 2 through 4 the responses requested. Do the same for each of the remaining rows.

1 ABILITY	2 EXPERIENCE DEMONSTRATING I HAVE ABILITY	3 EXPERIENCE DEMONSTRATING I DO NOT HAVE ABILITY	4 ABILITY LEVEL IN THIS AREA IS:				
			Very High	High	Aver-age	Fair	Poor
Managing/ Organizing							
Oral Communica-tion							
Written Communica-tion							
Supervising							
Planning							
Working under Pressure							
Leadership							
Following Instructions							

1 ABILITY	2 EXPERIENCE DEMONSTRATING I HAVE ABILITY	3 EXPERIENCE DEMONSTRATING I DO NOT HAVE ABILITY	4 ABILITY LEVEL IN THIS AREA IS:				
			Very High	High	Aver-age	Fair	Poor
Technical Skills							
Personal Relations							
Other Skills not covered—specify							

Discuss your listing with a partner. Consider the following:

- Have you overlooked some abilities?
- Have you categorized your abilities correctly? That is, are you under-rating or over-rating yourself?
- What abilities would you like to add to your repertoire?

INTERESTS

- *The purpose of this exercise is to increase your understanding of your interests in a number of career activity areas.*

Interests play an important role in career development. As a child, more than likely you responded to that familiar question, "What do you want to be when you grow up?" in terms of your interests. Whatever seemed most fascinating or glamorous at the time dictated your answer. As you grew older other things such as income and difficulty of work began to temper your interest. Nevertheless, interests remain an important part of career planning. One important criterion for selecting career activities is interest.

There are several standardized interest inventories which compare your interests with various groups of people. These can be taken at many college counseling and career planning centers. The inventory which follows has a different purpose. It is intended as an aid to revealing your interest reaction to 20 different kinds of career activities. The exercise has two parts. Do Part I now.

INTEREST INVENTORY

Part I: Listed below are twenty kinds of career activities in which you may or may not be interested. For each activity list five words that describe your feelings about the area. For example, if you enjoy public speaking you might list exciting, challenging, stimulating, fun and proud. On the other hand if you are fairly nervous before making any public speech and are not praised for your efforts, you might list scary, nerve racking, unrewarding, nervous and fearful. At this time ignore the short lines under the circle.

Public Speaking ◯

Business Management ◯

Direct Sales ◯

Military Activities ◯

Marketing

Technical Supervision

Science

Teaching

Agriculture

Art/Music/Drama

Recreational Leadership

Homemaking

Medical Service

Outdoor

Social Service

Organizational Activities

Religious Activities

Mechanical

Numerical

Planning

Now indicate whether each word you listed has a positive, negative, or neutral connotation to you. Score each response as follows: positive = +1; negative = -1; neutral = 0. Derive the total score for each area. The following is an example.

Public Speaking	+1 (circled) ← Total Score
Proud	+1
Challenging	+1
Rewarding	+1
Time Consuming	- 1
Draining	- 1

When you have finished scoring each activity, go to Part II.

Part II: On the following chart, list those areas that have a total score of +2 or above under Positive Areas and those that have -2 or below scores under Negative Areas. List the remainder under Neutral Areas.

POSITIVE AREAS

NEUTRAL AREAS

NEGATIVE AREAS

Review and share both parts of the Inventory. Discuss the following:

- What experiences have you had in each area that account for your positive or negative statements?
- Why might you anticipate dramatic changes in your interests in any of these areas?
- Were you surprised by any of the scores? Why?
- How might you use this information about your interests?
- Were there some areas in which you had no experience? If so, how were the words selected—societal stereotypes, peer discussions, second-hand experiences?
- How might you gain experience in areas in which you had no experience to determine whether your predicted interests hold up?

SOCIAL ISSUES

• *The purpose of this exercise is to increase your awareness of how career choices are affected by local, national and international issues.*

Current local, national and international events affect each of us in a different way. For example, in 1970 the environment and ecology movement was just beginning to emerge as an important national issue. The public was bombarded with facts, theories, scare stories, and testimonials concerning the movement and the problems associated with the environment. The public responded in many different ways—from making a concerted effort to recycle products to choosing environmental science as a major in college. It was difficult not to respond to the movement even if your response was resentment towards all the time and energy others spent talking about it. Take another example, the assassination of Robert Kennedy. How did you react? Was it anger, hurt, sadness, resignation? Some people reacted by deciding to work in VISTA or some similar organizations. Both of these events illustrate how societal issues and trends do have an impact on individual career development.

Consider another kind of social issue. Many college males do not believe that changing roles of women has much affect on them. It does, though, in very specific ways. First of all, equal opportunity for the sexes is being legislated. Thus, women have the legal right to apply for positions that have formerly been male-dominated; such as, telephone lineperson, mechanic, or traveling salesperson. Conversely, men are being considered as secretaries, elementary school teachers, and medical technicians. Affirmative Action also affects males. By Affirmative Action an employer means that if a male and a female applicant are competing for a position, it is highly likely that they will employ the female and upgrade her skills if necessary. It is obvious that these actions affect both men and women.

This exercise has you consider the impact current social events have on your own career development. The first step is to complete the "Impact of Social Issues" Data Sheet on the next page.

IMPACT OF SOCIAL ISSUES

Several current social issues are listed in Column 1. In the second column briefly describe what you believe to be the most important aspect of each issue. In the third column identify specific ways in which the issue affects your current behavior.

Social Trend or Issue	Important Aspects of Social Trend	Impact of Issue on My Behavior
Changing roles of men and women		
Racial and ethnic prejudice and discrimination		
Ecology, energy crisis, and overpopulation		
Counterculture movements		
Unemployment, underemployment, and job availability		
War		
(Your own choice—specify another social issue)		

Share the contents of the Data Sheet issue by issue, then discuss the following questions:

- In the next five years what social trend or issue do you predict will most influence your behavior?
- How do you think social issues influenced your parent's career development?
- How important are social issues in your career planning?

IMPORTANT OTHERS

- *The purpose of this exercise is to increase your understanding of how other people influence your behavior.*

Each of us is influenced by other people. The degree of influence varies from situation to situation and by our individual intellectual and emotional makeup. For example, some college students are highly influenced by their parents; their parents directly or indirectly select their college housing, choose their academic major, and pick their extra-curricular interests. On the other extreme, some students are determined to be on their own, independent of parental opinions and influence. These same students, though, might allow roommates or other friends to influence their behavior. Because being influenced by others is inevitable, it is important to understand how this influence affects your decision-making, especially career decisions.

Two considerations are important in thinking about the influence of others. First, who is the person having the influence; and second, what are the areas in which they have influence. In addition to the influential persons mentioned above, other influential people might include teachers, co-workers, employers, siblings, spouses, and other family members. The areas in which others influence include the entire realm of life experiences. During the college years, some of the most important areas include course selection, college major selection, dating behavior, study habits, entertainment selection, job choices, and financial spending habits.

The point is not that being influenced by another person is necessarily good or bad. It is simply important to know how you are influenced by others. Most everyone wants to be their own person at a decision-making time, even though others will have an influence. This exercise will assist you in considering how others currently affect your decision-making behavior.

YOU AND OTHERS

Seven decision-making areas are listed in Column 1. In the second column list people in your life that influence you in each decision-making area. In the third column use the scale below to rate the degree of influence of each person. In Column 4 note the form their influence takes. For example, is it direct or indirect, obvious or subtle, objective or biased?

The current influence of this person in this area is:

1 = very high
2 = high
3 = average
4 = low
5 = negligible

1. Decision-Making Areas	2. Influential Persons	3.	4. Form of Influence
Course Selection			
College Major Selection			
Dating Behavior			
Study Habits			
Entertainment Selection			
Job Choices			
Financial Spending Habits			

Share the contents of the Data Sheet and specifically discuss which people seem to influence you the most. Rank order from most to least influence each of these people. List these people below.

1.	6.
2.	7.
3.	8.
4.	9.
5.	10.

- Are you surprised at the results?
- Do you see yourself as more, or less, independent than you thought?
- In what areas would you like to have more influence from other people? In which areas would you like to have less?
- Reverse roles. Which people do you influence and how?

FEELING STATES

- *The purpose of this exercise is to increase your awareness of the feelings you experience and to provide an opportunity to discuss several aspects of emotional states.*

Emotional education is now becoming a part of many elementary school curricula. Children are assisted to understand that emotions are a natural part of living. In essence, the intent is to assure youngsters that emotional growth and understanding is as relevant to their development as academic learning.

Most of us were not exposed to a systematic study of emotional development in school, and thus it is probably not an overstatement to say that many people are afflicted with "emotional retardation." For many adults some emotional responses have been entirely extinguished (e.g., sorrow as expressed by crying in males). The recent popularity of encounter and growth groups is a societal response to the need and desire to explore what it means to be an emotional being.

This exercise starts with the premise that before you can deal effectively with feelings, you first must be able to describe them. People often lack the language to talk about feelings and emotions. This exercise gives you practice in describing your feelings. For example, suppose a wife is hurt because her husband did not compliment the meal she prepared especially for him. She is faintly aware of this, but is unable to say, "I prepared that meal because I thought you would enjoy it, and I guess I was hoping you would comment on it. I'm just a little hurt, but I feel better because I mentioned it." Because she does not make the statement, her emotions go from hurt to anger to resentment to depression, to anger and around again. She ends up on an emotional merry-go-round. Being able to identify the emotions you are experiencing and having a language readily available to use to express the emotion can often be helpful in an emotional situation.

Knowing your feelings and how they affect you is an important part of career development. For example, some jobs by their very nature increase the chance that you will experience rejection and resentment. If these feelings are especially difficult for you to cope with, you might want to reconsider taking such a job. Becoming more aware of how your feelings affect you can be useful information in making career decisions and plans.

FEELING STATES

Listed below in Column 1 are some common feelings experienced by many people. Complete columns as directed.

Feeling	Note two ways you express each feeling	I experience this feeling:					Describe the last time you experienced this feeling
		Very Often	Often	Some-times	Sel-dom	Hard-ly ever	
Sadness							
Hurt							
Anger							
Love							
Frustra-tion							
Con-fusion							
Trust							
Resent-ment							
Rejec-tion							

Review and share the contents of the Data Sheet. Discuss the following:

- Which feelings do you experience the most? Which do you experience the least?
- Of those feelings you experience a great deal, which do you consider to be negative emotions? How well do you deal with these negative emotions?
- Are specific situations (combination of people, places and things) more likely to produce certain feelings in you?
- Try to list several career activities which would probably promote pleasant feelings for you. What occupations would tend to generate unpleasant feelings?

HIGH POINTS

You have probably produced a good deal of information about yourself while doing the exercises in this section. Hopefully you increased your self-understanding. Want to find out? If you do, try the following. Review your Data Sheets from each exercise and note the answer to the following question regarding each Data Sheet.

What is the most important discovery you made about yourself regarding:

Abilities	Social Issues
Interests	Values
Feeling States	Important Others

OCCUPATIONS
3

• *The purpose of this section is to learn an occupational classification system and examine the relationship between college resources and occupations.*

CLASSIFYING JOBS

In order to find or make your place in the world of work, it is important to know something about work and how it is organized. In technical jargon, the world of work is known as the "national occupational structure." There is no way (nor any reason) to know about each of the 40,000 occupations which exist in this country. With a little effort, however, you can develop a useful working knowledge of the occupational structure.

First, let us give some order to that huge collection of occupations. Following are two lists. List A consists of 8 definitions. Each definition describes a category of work based on focus of activity. List B consists of 8 work focus labels. Your task is to match the labels in List B with the definitions in List A.

List A

I. ____________ These occupations are primarily concerned with serving and attending to the personal tastes, needs, and welfare of other persons.

II. ____________ These occupations are primarily concerned with the face-to-face sale of commodities, investments, real estate, and services.

III. ____________ These are the managerial and white collar jobs in business, industry, and government, the occupations concerned primarily with the organization and efficient functioning of commercial enterprises and of government activities.

IV. ____________ This group includes occupations concerned with the production, maintenance, and transportation of commodities and utilities.

V. ____________ These occupations are primarily concerned with the cultivation, preservation, and gathering of crops, of marine or inland water resources, of mineral resources, of forest products, and of other natural resources, and with animal husbandry.

VI. ____________ These are the occupations primarily concerned with scientific theory and its application under specified circumstances, other than technology.

VII. ____________ These occupations are primarily concerned with the preservation and transmission of the general cultural heritage.

VIII. ____________ These occupations include those primiarily concerned with the use of special skills in the creative arts and in the field of entertainment.

List B

Technology	General Culture	Service	Organization
Science	Outdoor	Arts & Entertainment	Business Contact

Now turn the page and compare your responses with the answer key.

The classification system illustrated here is from Roe, Anne, *The Psychology of Occupations*, John Wiley and Sons, New York, 1956.

ANSWER KEY

I. Service
II. Business Contact
III. Organization
IV. Technology
V. Outdoor
VI. Science
VII. General Culture
VIII. Arts & Entertainment

You now know that all occupations can be group according to 8 categories, each of which represents a primary focus of activity. Sure, there is some overlap. The categories are not perfect. Even so, they are still useful. Let's test them.

On the following page is a list of 22 occupations, and a form with 8 columns, one for each of the occupational categories. Your task is to read each item on the list and enter it in the appropriate column.

EIGHT OCCUPATIONAL GROUPS

Put each of the following occupations into one of the groups listed below.

Law Clerk
Certified Public Accountant
Miner
Auctioneer
Occupational Therapist
Athlete
Aviators
Peddlers
Public Relations Specialist
Personal Counselor
Truck Driver
Veterinarian
Editor
Window Decorator
Owner of Dry Cleaners
Lumberjack
Taxi Driver
Warehouse Foreman
Creative Artist
Typist
Promoter
Barber
Mechanic
U.S. President
Chiropractor
Ad Writer
Librarian
Automobile Salesman
Museum Curator
Applied Scientist
Police Detective
Messenger Boy
Laborer
Greeting Card Illustrator
Gardener
Veterinarian Hospital Attendant
Medical Technical Assistant
Elevator Operator
Chief Engineer
Landscape Architect
College Professor
Farm County Agent

Service	Business Contact	Organization	Technology

Outdoor	Science	General Culture	Arts & Entertainment

When you are finished, please turn the page.

ANSWER KEY FOR OCCUPATIONAL GROUPS

Now check your placements with this key. Make appropriate changes. You may disagree with our categorization. That's fine—the system isn't perfect.

Service	Business Contact	Organization	Technology
Police Detective	Auctioneer	Messenger Boy	Truck Driver
Counselors	Public Relations Counselors	U.S. President	Chief Engineer
Taxi Drivers	Peddlers	Typist	Laborers
Barbers	Promoters	Certified Public Accountant	Applied Scientist
Occupational Therapist	Automobile Salesman	Owner of Dry Cleaners	Mechanic
Elevator Operators		Warehouse Foreman	Aviators

Outdoor	Science	General Culture	Arts & Entertainment
Landscape Architect	Veterinarians	Librarian	Window Decorator
Lumberjack	Museum Curator	Law Clerk	Athlete
County Agent	Chiropractor	Editors	Greeting Card Illustrator
Gardener	Technical Assistants	College Professor	Ad Writer
Miners	Veterinary Hospital Attendant		Creative Artist

Begin the next phase of the exercise.

We can now add a second dimension to the classification system, that of **Level** of work. Level refers to the amount of responsibility entailed in a job. The following six levels have been identified.

1. PROFESSIONAL AND MANAGERIAL 1: INDEPENDENT RESPONSIBILITY. This Level includes not only the innovators and creators, but also the top managerial and administrative people, as well as those professional persons who have independent responsibility in important respects.
2. PROFESSIONAL AND MANAGERIAL 2: The distinction between this Level and Level 1 is primarily one of degree. Genuine autonomy may be present but with narrower or less significant responsibilities than in Level 1.
3. SEMI-PROFESSIONAL AND SMALL BUSINESS. The criteria suggested here are: (a) Low-level responsibility for others. (b) Application of policy, or determination for self only (as in managing a small business). (c) Education—high school plus technical school or the equivalent.
4. SKILLED. Skilled occupations require apprenticeship or other special training or experience.
5. SEMI-SKILLED. These occupations require some training and experience but markedly less than the occupations in Level 4.
6. UNSKILLED. These occupations require no special training or education and not much more ability than is needed to follow simple directions and to engage in simple repetitive actions.

Your next task is to assign a level of work to each occupation you categorized on page 33. Write the appropriate level number in front of each occupation you entered on the chart.

Now check your responses with the list on the following page.

ANSWER KEY FOR OCCUPATIONAL GROUPS & LEVELS

Service	Business Contact	Organization	Technology
Police Detective 3	Auctioneer 4	Messenger Boy 6	Truck Driver 5
Counselor 1	Public Relations Counselor 2	U.S. President 1	Chief Engineer 1
Taxi Driver 5	Peddlers 5	Typist 5	Laborers 6
Barbers 4	Promoters 1	Certified Public Accountant 2	Applied Scientist 2
Occupational Therapist 2	Automobile Salesman 3	Owner of Dry Cleaners 3	Mechanic 4
Elevator Operator 6		Warehouse Foreman 4	Aviators 3

Outdoor	Science	General Culture	Arts & Entertainment
Landscape Architect 2	Veterinarians 2	Librarian 3	Window Decorator 5
Lumberjack 6	Museum Curator 1	Law Clerk 4	Athlete 2
County Agent 3	Chiropractor 3	Editors 2	Greeting Card Illustrator 5
Gardener 5	Technical Assistants 4	College Professor 1	Ad Writer 3
Miners 4	Veterinary Hospital Attendant 5		Creative Artist 1

You have now learned a two-way occupational classification system. "So what," you may be wondering. "What use is the system?"

Well, for a start, you may have already identified certain areas of work which have more appeal to you than others. If that is true, you have begun to sharpen the focus of your career planning. You may also have developed a new awareness of work which you may want to explore. It also may have occurred to you that certain **levels** as well as categories of work may be more appealing than others. We'll return to the classification system later.

EDUCATION AND JOBS

Consider another aspect of work. There is an obvious relationship between amount of education and occupations. For example, rank the following occupations from that requiring the greatest amount of education to that requiring the least. Assign number 1 to the occupation requiring the greatest amount of formal education.

________	High School Teacher
________	Brain Surgeon
________	Welder
________	Laborer
________	X-Ray Lab Technician

Obvious. Okay, now try to rank the following occupations in the same manner

________	Bank President
________	Sales Manager
________	Commercial Airline Pilot
________	Congressman
________	Inventor

Tough, if not impossible to do, isn't it? Some occupations have minimal requirements in terms of amount of education. You've probably seen job listings which say "high school graduates only" or "college degree required."

There are other occupations which have specific educational requirements. Try to list a few below:

If you listed occupations such as engineer, physician, pharmacist, accountant, and nurse, you have the right idea. Career planning regarding these kinds of occupations usually must start fairly early in one's college years.

There are other occupations which have much more flexibility in regard to educational preparation, but which still require a credential such as a license, or certificate. List several such occupations below.

Examples that come to mind are detective, real estate salesperson, insurance salesperson, and radio engineer. These occupations have considerable flexibility in regard to career planning. For some of these, employers provide on-the-job training or special training programs. When this is the case, certain important options remain open to both the individual and the employer. Consider the following example.

The Bet-Your-Life insurance company has an opening for a new agent. They have narrowed their choices down to X and Y. X has a B.S. in business, which includes 3 courses in insurance. X is quiet, somewhat uncomfortable in social situations, and likes to have activities structured by someone else. Y, on the other hand, has a B.A. in English, is outgoing, enjoys being with people, and is a "self starter" capable of self-direction.

Which one will get the position? ☐
If the insurance company has a training program, we'll bet on Y, even though X has specific preparation for the position.

Thus, the "requirements" for a great many occupations are a mixture of specific and general education on the one hand, and personal characteristics on the other. When this is the case, the relationship between college courses and occupational requirements is more or less vague. In such instances students must take the initiative in assembling their own preparation program. That is, the resources are there, but you must put them together. Imagine that you are attending a college which does not offer specific programs or "majors" for the following occupations.

Museum Manager

Overseas Sales Representative

Television Station Manager

Industrial Training Specialist

Bureau of Indian Affairs Administrator

Environmental Protection Specialist

After each occupation note the various college departments in which you could probably find courses to build a preparation program.

Compare your notes with ours on the next page.

Museum Manager—fine arts, business, political science, history, anthropology

Overseas Sales Representative— business, foreign language, history, political science, economics

T.V. Station Manager—business, drama, education, journalism

Industrial Training Specialist—business, education, psychology, engineering

Bureau of Indian Affairs Administration—anthropology, sociology, business, history, education

Environmental Protection Specialist —sciences, business admistration, political science, journalism

So, even though your college may not have an organized program which suits your interest, it is likely that you can, by knowing and using the institution's resources, develop one for yourself.

JOB CONDITIONS

Now, one final idea which relates to the occupational classification system we looked at earlier. Throughout this exercise we have essentially viewed occupation in terms of job "content." There is another aspect of occupations—or any activity, for that matter—which you are well aware of, and that is the conditions under which activities are done.

We can illustrate the content-conditions idea by looking at the basis upon which you select courses. Obviously, you selected many of your courses on the basis of the concepts, information, and skills with which they were concerned. You were interested in course content. Most likely, however, you were influenced from time to time by the conditions under which courses were offered. Important conditions include the instructor's personality, his examination procedures, class size, and time of day offered. The distinction is not simply one of good and bad conditions but, more important, one of different conditions. In regard to course conditions, for example, some people prefer frequent examinations to provide them with a basis for monitoring their progress as they go through the course. Others, in contrast, would prefer to skip the inconvenience of preparing for weekly quizzes and place all of their energy in studying for finals.

The concepts of content and condition hold equally well for occupations. We can easily be misled into making an unsatisfying job selection because of considering only content or only condition of work. Both are important. To illustrate this point, consider the occupation of salesperson. In the box below, list 3 or 4 words which describe the daily content experiences of a sales clerk working in a one-person general store in a small farm community. Then list several words which describe probable working conditions.

JOB CONTENT

JOB CONDITIONS

Now make a list of experiences for a sales clerk in a large New York antique shop.

JOB CONTENT

JOB CONDITIONS

As your lists demonstrate—the same occupation, salesperson, can be very different depending on the conditions of work. Many times the conditions of work may be more important to an individual than the actual job content.

More than just the specific work environment is involved in the conditions idea. For example, the general physical and political environment in which one performs an occupation can have as great an impact on general lifestyle as the specific condition and content of work. To demonstrate this to yourself, note probable conditions in the following chart for each of the two jobs just described.

	Occupations	
Environmental Conditions	Salesperson in Rural General Store	Salesperson in City Shoppe
Transportation Options		
Recreation Available		
Housing Options		
Medical Resources		

The example is a simple one, but the principle applies: Choosing an occupation and a place in which to do it will have a major impact on the total lifestyle you will lead.

You now have a conceptual framework for looking at occupational information. We urge you to take the next step, and use it. Section 7 lists many sources of occupational information that will assist you in narrowing your own occupational choices.

LIFESTYLES
4

- *The purpose of this section is to assist you to clarify several ways in which your values may significantly influence your lifestyle during the next ten years.*

Lifestyle is a term currently used by many people but it is found, as of this writing, in only one dictionary (*Webster's New Collegiate Dictionary*, 1973). Lifestyle is defined as "an individual's typical way of life." In order to learn what the term means to those who use it, we surveyed a small sample of people, asking them, "What does the word 'lifestyle' mean to you?" Among the responses were the following:

- living one's life according to one's own standards
- a set of values concerning living and working conditions
- how each individual lives his day-to-day existence and this varies according to the people and conditions with which you are involved
- an attitude toward life values shown in the way one lives one's life
- the way in which one chooses to live as it relates to other people
- the way one chooses to spend one's resources, which include time, money, and energy

Quite a variety from a small number of people. What is your definition of lifestyle? Write it below.

Each of us, of course, is entitled to our own definition. For purposes of this exercise, however, we ask that you consider lifestyle to refer to the values, occupational and leisure activities, relationships and material possessions which characterize any given individual. Your task in this exercise is to project ten years into the future then describe what your lifestyle might be like. Use the remainder of this and the following page to write your projection. Included in your description might be answers to the following questions.

- Will you be living with anyone? If so, under what conditions?
- How many, if any children will you have? By what philosophy will you be raising them?
- Will you have lived in the same community for a long time or have moved frequently?
- Will you be working? At what kind of occupation? Will you be satisfied?
- What will you be "into"? Leisure activities? Political activities? Work?
- For what will you spend your money? What kind of house will you live in? What kind of material possessions will you have?
- What will be the chief sources of self-fulfillment in your life?

Your 10 Year Projected Lifestyle

Also use the following page.

Lifestyle Projection Continued

Review what you have written carefully, and then circle the appropriate response to each of the following statements.

1. Living the lifestyle I have described, I will have to be earning: (based on current standards)

   over $16,000 $10,000–$16,000 below $10,000

2. The amount of time required to raise the number of children by the methods I prefer will be:

   great average minimal

3. The amount of money required to raise the number of children by the methods I prefer will be:

   great average minimal

4. The amount of time it will take to pursue the leisure/cultural/political activities I desire will be:

   great average minimal

5. The amount of money required to pursue these leisure/cultural/political activities will be:

   great average minimal

6. The amount of training beyond college required by the kind of occupation I projected will be:

   2 or more years 1–2 more years none

7. The number of hours per week I will be working in my projected occupation will be:

   50+ 40 20-39 1-19

8. In doing the kind of work I described, the level of responsibilities will be:

   major average minimal

9. In the lifestyle I have described I will:

   be fairly well established in one community

   have lived in the same place for the last 3 years

   be moving from place to place

10. The amount of time it will take to achieve the relationship(s) I have described will be:

    great average minimal

Now review your responses to the previous ten statements and consider the following questions:

- Are you describing a lifestyle that takes an above average amount of time, money, or energy? If so, what problems might be encountered in such a lifestyle and how would you deal with these?
- Are you describing a lifestyle that takes a minimal amount of time, money, or energy? If so, what might be missing from your life?
- Are there inconsistencies between portions of your lifestyle description? Consider the following examples that point up inconsistencies:
  - A person indicating an annual income of $10,000 and describing expensive leisure activities.
  - Someone stating they will probably work 50+ hours a week and also intending to spend a great deal of time in leisure pursuits.
  - A person describing spending great amounts of time each in: raising children, achieving satisfactory relationships, leisure pursuits, their work, and in achieving accomplishments.
- If you have any inconsistencies or discrepancies in your statement, how might you deal with these?
- How difficult was it to predict ten years ahead?
- In light of this future lifestyle analysis, are there things you might do now to prepare for the future?

DECISIONS
5

• *The purpose of this section is to describe and practice a rational decision-making procedure.*

Each of our careers involves a series of decisions, many of which are difficult. You no doubt made decisions such as what courses to take in high school, how much time and energy you would devote to studying for these, whether to go to college, which college to attend, and what major to follow. Sometime in the future, if not already, you will be faced with deciding about such things as taking a job, getting married, having children, and changing jobs.

At this point, however, you probably are most concerned with those decisions regarding college, jobs, and the transition from one to the other. These are often difficult decisions because a great deal of uncertainty can be involved. In this sense, decisions involve predictions in that a decision implies a cause and effect. For example, when I decide to major in a professional school rather than liberal arts, it can be inferred that I am predicting, "a professional degree will result in more employment opportunities than a liberal arts degree." If, when choosing between offers from Xerox and Hometown Enterprises, I select Xerox, one can infer that I am predicting, "I will have greater opportunity for advancement with Xerox than with Hometown Enterprises."

If you knew what you wanted, and if you were certain that A would lead to B, then decisions of whether or not to do A would not be difficult. Often, however, you are not sure of what you want and, especially with regard to career decisions, you usually are not certain that A will lead to B. One means of reducing uncertainty regarding decisions (or at least clarifying the extent of uncertainty which exists) is to use the rational decision-making procedure illustrated in this section.

STATING GOALS

Probably the most difficult part of decision making is coming up with a clear statement of what it is that you want. Thus, it should be helpful to examine the business of stating goals for decisions before moving to a consideration of rational decision-making procedures. A goal is not the decision. A goal describes what you want. The decision is concerned with choosing a means of obtaining what you want.

It may seem obvious that you need to know your goals when making a decision. Yet, many people tend to state goals with such ambiguity as to obscure many possible alternative means to achieving them. Perhaps even worse, vaguely stated goals can create the feeling that there are an almost infinite number of alternatives, thus, overwhelming the decision maker into a state of decision-making paralysis. For example, if you state you want to have a job where you are "working with people" (a commonly stated career goal) you might be saying something significant about the kind of occupation you do not want, such as a forest ranger in a lookout tower or a night watchman. But, you are saying little that will assist you to choose from the myriad of occupations which involve "working with people." That could be anything from prostitute to president.

What, then, is an adequate goal statement? First of all, a goal statement should be specific about what you want. It should provide some clear indication of the conditions which would need to exist for you to be able to say that your goal had been met. Try applying this criterion to the following eight goal statements. Check those which meet the criterion of specifying conditions.

_ 1. By the time I am 25, I want to be independent; I want to be living apart from family and paying all my own bills.

_ 2. When I have children, I want to feel that I am ready financially.

_ 3. I want to have landed a job in sales or personnel prior to graduation.

_ 4. I want to make a difference in the work that I do. This has always been important to me.

_ 5. I want to have at least 30 days vacation per year after I have been working for five years.

_ 6. When I come home from work at night, I want to feel that I accomplished something.

_ 7. I need a lifestyle that will permit me several hours a day alone doing my own thing.

_ 8. Most of all, I want an education.

If you checked only statements 1, 3, and 5 as meeting the criterion of specificity, you have the idea. Statement 2 gives us no hint about what it would take to be "financially ready." Statement 4 communicates nothing and 6, 7, and 8 are nearly as vague.

In addition to specificity, statements of goals should indicate time conditions when appropriate. This is illustrated in the preceding list. Note statements 1, 2, 3, and 5, each of which indicates a time by which the goal is to be achieved. In each example time limits are included. The amount of time within which a goal is to be gained can be as important as the goal itself. For example, my goal may be to run my own business. However, I don't want to spend my life striving for this goal. In fact, if I haven't achieved the goal by the time I am 35, then forget it. In this example, stating the time limitations of my goal clarifies my intentions.

RATIONAL DECISION MAKING

In the remainder of this section we will illustrate a rational decision-making procedure. To begin, it should be helpful to provide an illustration of a rational decision-making process. A decision regarding life insurance will serve our needs. In this situation the decision maker (customer) usually has a simple goal: to provide adequate financial resources for the family should he or she die. The salesperson first asks you to clarify your goal—to define what is meant by "adequate financial resources." The definition is neat and clean—so many dollars per year, decreasing each year according to the expected independence of children. The salesperson then gathers information about your existing financial resources such as retirement income, social security, savings, and investments. He then gives all of this information regarding your goal and resources to a computer for analysis. He returns in a week, and presents you with the results of the analysis. He offers you three alternatives. Plan A provides maximum protection, completely achieving your goal. Plan B adequately meets your goals if your spouse is gainfully employed, and Plan C is a cheapie thrown in to salvage something out of his sales effort even if you don't care enough about your family to provide them with adequate protection. The decision to be made is clear. You know both the cost and benefits of each plan. Take your choice. Uncertainty exists, but uncertainty accompanies all significant decisions.

Nine Steps and a Worksheet

Now let's apply the same rational decision-making procedure to more complex career decisions. The procedure consists of nine steps and involves using the Career Decision Worksheet on Pages 52-53. It will be instructive to refer to the worksheet as you read through the following description.

1. **Stating a goal.** Describe the goal of your decision. Be as specific as possible. Be sure that you identify the basic problem, and not one of the alternative solutions. For example, "should I go to summer school" is not a basic problem. It is one alternative to "How can I best spend the summer." Write a clear and specific statement of your goal in space 1. Work on one goal at a time. If your analysis has resulted in several goals, select the most important one.

2. **Generating alternatives.** List in space 2 every possible alternative means you can think of for achieving the goal. If you can't think of alternatives, ask others for suggestions and seek out information whenever possible (see Chapter 7). Regardless of how impractical some alternatives appear list them anyway. Hold off on value judgments.

3. **Evaluating alternatives.** Now review your list of alternatives. Combine those which appear redundant, and eliminate any which are so much in conflict with your values that you can't accept them.

4. **Estimating needed resources.** In space 3 note the resources needed to implement each alternative. Resources are those things, people, facts, money, skills, and anything else that will be required to implement a particular alternative. Don't overlook personal resources such as persistence and self-confidence. This step often requires obtaining information regarding some or all of the alternatives.

5. **Evaluating resources.** Eliminate (cross out) alternatives for which resources are clearly unavailable or too difficult to acquire.

6. **Identifying risks.** In space 4 note the risks and any undesirable aspects entailed in each remaining alternative. Risks in this case refer to what you might lose by pursuing each alternative, and include factors such as self-esteem and relationships as well as material items.

7. **Risk rating.** Now use space 5 to rate each remaining alternative according to your willingness to accept the risks or undesirable aspects involved. Use the following scale:

1 = Risk acceptable
2 = Risk mostly acceptable—some reservations
3 = Risk mostly unacceptable—very uncomfortable with it
4 = Risk totally unacceptable

Rule out all alternatives rated 4.

8. **Deciding by risk.** Now, if you want to make a decision with minimum risk select the alternative means which has the most acceptable risk level and for which resources can be obtained. (There may be more than one alternative with the most acceptable risk rating. When this is true, go on to step 9.)

or

9. **Deciding by preference.** If low risk is not the most important consideration, then do an "alternatives preference ranking." To do this, first record the bases or criteria of preference in space 6. (Preference criteria can range from "impact on others" to "it feels good.") Then use space 7 to rank the alternatives according to your preference and without regard to the level of risk involved. Now choose the alternative which has the highest preference ranking *and* an acceptable risk rating.

CAREER DECISION WORKSHEET

1. Goal:
What should I do after graduation that I will find personally fulfilling?

2. ALTERNATIVES	**3. RESOURCES**	
	Skills	**Money**

CAREER DECISION WORKSHEET

7. Preference Criteria:
An alternative that will have an impact on others and personally challenge me.

NEEDED		4. RISKS AND UNDESIRABLE ASPECTS	5. Risk Rating	6. Pref-erence
Personal	Other			

An Example

The following example illustrates the steps in the decision-making process.

Kathy Myers is 21 and just beginning her senior year in college. She is majoring in psychology, a discipline she's enjoyed very much. Her grade point average is 3.2 and she has taken several classes on a pass–no pass basis. Kathy has begun to do some serious thinking about what she is going to do next year and has decided to complete the Career Decision Worksheet.

On the personal side, Kathy has been seriously involved with Bob for over a year. However, at this time she does not want to let this particular relationship dictate her future plans; she does not want to get tied down to one person at this time. Kathy's parents are fairly achievement oriented, and they would like her either to go to graduate school or take a position in some career field. She respects their opinions but feels free to do what she thinks is best.

Since high school Kathy has had a strong interest in environmental/ecological concerns and has been a member and organizer of several environmental projects during her college years. Other outside interests have included making pottery and leather goods. During college Kathy has worked part-time as a typist in several of the campus offices.

Kathy's thinking is described below and summarized on the Career Decision Worksheet:

STEP 1: Stating a goal. After some consideration, Kathy outlined her question as, "What should I do after graduation that I will find personally fulfilling?" Kathy realized that the word fulfilling was not very descriptive, but by that she meant an activity that provided her with experiences that would assist in her personal growth or an activity in which she worked with other people in a problem-solving situation.

STEP 2: Generating alternatives. Kathy listed six alternatives. She realized this list was probably not exhaustive (for example she could join the army or a convent) but her list did contain a fair number of alternatives to consider.

STEP 3: Evaluating alternatives. Kathy reviewed her list of alternatives and found none in conflict with her values.

STEP 4: Identifying needed resources. The next step was to determine what kind of resources would be needed for each alternative. This took a lot of time and effort on her part. She found that it was necessary to imagine what it would be like to live each of the alternatives before she could identify all the resources that would be needed. The most difficult resources to pinpoint were the personal-emotional resources that would be required if each alternative became a reality. To do this she imagined the kind of interactions and negotiations that might occur with each alternative, and, then, based on past experience, she predicted how she might react in the situations. On that basis she predicted what emotional resources would be needed. The list that she developed is shown on the Worksheet.

STEP 5: Evaluating resources. The next task was to eliminate alternatives for which there were inadequate resources or the resources were too difficult to obtain. After reviewing the list, Kathy decided there was really only one alternative, travel in the U.S. or Europe, for which the resources were not available. At this point Kathy felt she did not have the skills and desire to be out on her own as much as would be required in a traveling lifestyle. One other resource would be difficult to obtain and that was enough money to finance graduate school. But she thought a combination of borrowing from her parents, a summer and part-time job, and a loan would make it possible to obtain, so she did not eliminate the alternative.

STEP 6: Identifying risks. In the next phase of the decision making Kathy noted the risks and undesirable aspects entailed in each decision. Again she found that she had to mentally estimate what would be involved. Her list of risks and undesirable aspects is contained on the Worksheet.

STEP 7: Risk rating. As the next step Kathy rated the risks for each alternative, using the 4-point scale:

1 = Risk acceptable
2 = Risk mostly acceptable—some reservations
3 = Risk mostly unacceptable—very uncomfortable with it
4 = Risk totally unacceptable

As you can see on the chart, Kathy had no 4 ratings.

STEP 8: Deciding by risk. Kathy still had 5 alternatives for which she could probably obtain the resources and which had acceptable risks. If she had been seeking a low risk decision then at this point she would have rejected the two alternatives with number 3 risk ratings, and decided among the last three alternatives. However, because she was not primarily interested in a low risk, she was willing to consider all of the 5 remaining alternatives.

STEP 9: Deciding by preference. She ranked the five alternatives in terms of her preference. The criteria she used were: (a) personal challenge and (b) impact on others. Her ranking is noted in the last column on the form. Kathy felt going to graduate school in and of itself would have little immediate impact on others, and she realized that was really important to her now. Working for the federal government, she felt, would not be challenging enough. As shown, she ranked management trainee positions as the preferred alternative.

1. Goal:
What should I do after graduation that I will find personally fulfilling?

2. ALTERNATIVES	3. RESOURCES	
	Skills	Money
A. Go to Graduate School in Psychology	–Ability to do graduate level work –Would have to be able to find out information about different graduate programs and complete application procedures	–Tuition plus room and board plus other expenses would be $2,000 a year
B. Join ACTION and go in the Peace Corps	–Ability to complete application procedure –Ability to adapt to new cultural situation	–Would earn minimal income but no financial outlay needed
C. Interview for Management trainee Positions in Business	–Would have to have effective interviewing and job search skills	–Would need money to relocate, get established, and buy clothes
D. Interview for Semi-skilled Positions (such as Typist, Bank Teller, etc.) and devote most of Energy to Environmental Action Groups	–Have needed skills for this alternative	–Would need minimal money to get started
E. Go into Federal or State Government Work	–Would have to have effective interviewing and test taking skills	–Would need money to relocate and get established
F. Travel around the U.S and Europe alone	–Would have to be able to get a series of part-time jobs –Would have to be able to deal with many new situations	–Would have to be able to earn enough money to live on

7. Preference Criteria:
An alternative that will have an impact on others and personally challenge me.

NEEDED		4. RISKS AND UNDESIRABLE ASPECTS	5. Risk Rating	6. Preference
Personal	Other			
—Would have to be able to tolerate 1-2 more years in school		—Might be just as unemployable with a master's degree	3	4
—Ability to tolerate loneliness —Would have to deal with parents'/boyfriend's objections		—Might terminate relationship with boyfriend —Might seem like a wasted 2 years	3	2
—Would have to reconcile my image of business with what I experienced in the job —Would have to deal with boyfriend's objections		—Might become "too materialistic" —Might terminate relationship with boyfriend	2	1
—Would have to deal with parent's objections		—Might feel like all my efforts in environmental action are fruitless and I'm stuck in a clerical job.	2	3
—Would have to deal with boyfriend's objections		—Might become part of "the establishment" —Might terminate relationship with boyfriend	2	5
~~—Would have to deal with parent's objections —Would have to deal with some loneliness~~				

The best way to learn about rational decision making is to use it. For practice, select a decision that you are currently working on and complete the blank Career Decision Worksheet on page 52. After completing the Worksheet, consider the following:

- Did you take into consideration more variables by using the rational decision-making procedure?
- What are the advantages to using this procedure?

IMPLEMENTING DECISIONS
6

- *The purpose of this section is to describe several methods for implementing decisions.*

The real payoff from a decision comes when you put it into action. In fact, many people would claim that a decision becomes important only when some action has been taken. Often, however, putting a decision into effect is not easy. We can procrastinate, find all kinds of reasons for putting off the desired action, and then sooner or later rationalize that it is simply too late and forget the whole matter.

In this section we will describe several ways for overcoming those kinds of implementation problems. None of these procedures can guarantee that you will achieve the goals you have set for yourself; they can, however, be helpful aids in working toward career satisfaction.

If you have progressed successfully through this program, you should be at a point where you:

1) can accurately describe some of your abilities, interests, and values,
2) have an awareness of career possibilities in general and know how to obtain more specific information,
3) have considered the concept of lifestyle from several perspectives, and
4) have practiced a rational decision-making procedure.

Hopefully, you have made some important career decisions. Whatever those decisions may be, implementation is crucial. It should be helpful to reflect for a moment regarding the reasons why important decisions often never get off the ground. There are many reasons, but the following seem especially important.

1. We don't know where to begin.
2. There seem to be so many things to do at once that confusion soon reigns and renders us immobile.
3. The amount of time between when we begin and achieving our goal is so great that we become discouraged and lose interest.

These are the implementation problems with which we will deal in this section. Stated in positive terms they are:

—Getting started
—Planning
—Maintaining motivation

GETTING STARTED

Getting started towards implementing a career decision is the first phase of making a plan. One effective means of starting is to do a quick overview of the kinds of things which you will do to implement your decision between now and some target date in the future. The "Implementation Overview" form illustrated below was designed to help you with this task. To begin, enter today's date. (What's past is past—it's the future that you are concerned about now.) Next note the career decision you have made. What have you decided to do? You may want to record the larger goal of your decision, or perhaps only its first phase. For example, while your larger decision may be to complete a one-year training course, implementation may be more effective if you concentrate on completing the first term of study. Whether you decide to consider the total decision or some smaller aspect of it, set a target date by which you want to have finished your implementation tasks. Then, without regard to any time sequence, note your responses to the several categories on the form. When you have completed this exercise, you have begun implementing your decision. If the decision is a relatively simple one, completing the "Implementation Overview" may be all that is needed.

In the case of more complex decisions, you may want to translate the notes made on Overview into a more specific implementation plan.

IMPLEMENTATION OVERVIEW

Today's Date	Career Decision	Target Date

Information to be Sought	Money and Personal Resources Required
Skills and Abilities Needed	**Helpful Experiences Needed**
Arrangements to be Made	**Other Decisions to be Made**

PLANNING

A critical aspect of planning as we are using the term is that of committing the plan to paper. Generally speaking, a written plan is more effective than one unwritten. Writing tends to clarify, add specificity, and help identify gaps or missing parts.

A typical implementation plan consists of a detailed list of steps to be taken in carrying out a decision. These steps are listed in the logical sequence by which they might be accomplished. To facilitate planning, it is useful to estimate the amount of time for accomplishing each step in the plan. For example, let's return to Kathy whose decision to obtain a management trainee position in business was considered in Section V. Her implementation .plan might look as follows in column 2.

Implementation Plan

Action to be Taken	Estimated Time
1. Complete credential file	2 weeks
2. Complete a resume.	2 weeks
3. Sharpen interview skills.	1 week
4. Develop list of potential employers.	2 weeks
5. Research those employers.	2 weeks
6. Do job interviews.	6 weeks

Some career changes are relatively complex and may be difficult to plan using simple lists. In such instances, when several things must be done simultaneously, the use of a time line can be helpful. A time line provides for a two-dimensional display of the activities to be done. The visual display of the overlapping activities helps many people develop a clearer understanding of the various aspects of their plan. The following example illustrates the use of a time line in the case of Kathy.

Time Line for Implementation Plan

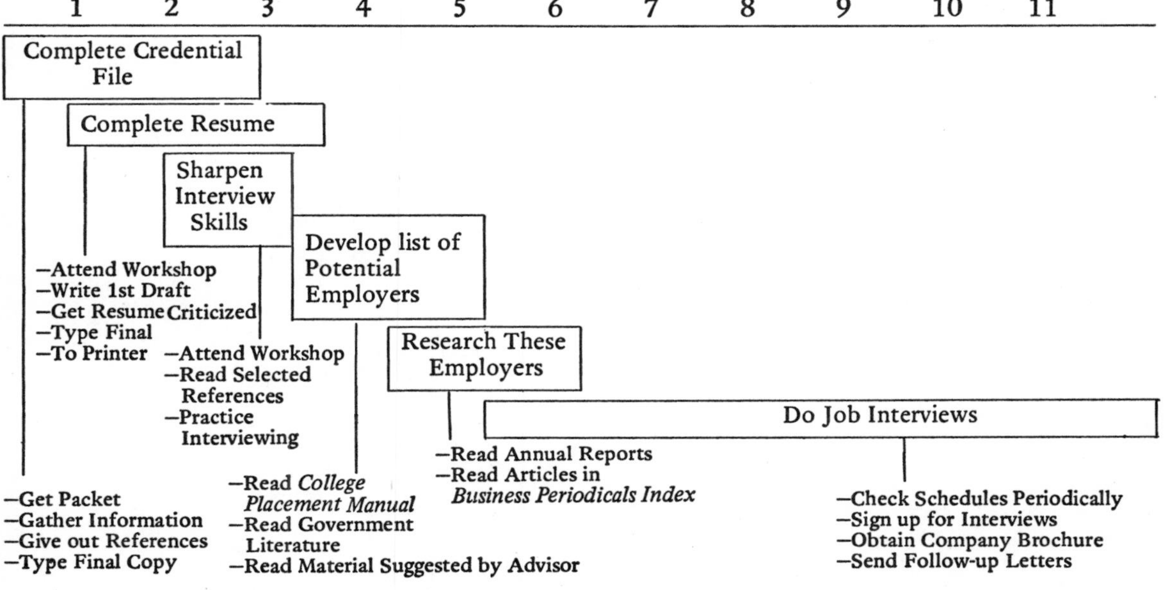

In developing an implementation plan, it helps to be as precise as possible about what each step involves. One way to be precise is to note the action to be taken at each step in the plan. In other words, use a verb in describing each step. Also, try to break each step into smaller parts. For example, if one of your steps is "gather information about employers" a more precise description of what is involved might read:

1. **List** employers of interest
2. **Write** for company brochures
3. **Read** professional journals for articles about companies of interest
4. **Request** interviews with representatives of companies
5. **Talk** to an employee of each company for more information

Keeping in mind these two principles—specification of **action** to be taken and **breaking an action down** into its component parts—follow the instruction below for completing an implementation plan for a decision you have made.

- List all of the tasks which must be taken to implement your decision in Column 1 (Action to be Taken) on the Implementation Plan form.
- In Column 2 estimate the amount of time necessary to complete each task.
- If your plan involves tasks which can be done simultaneously, then display it on the Time Line chart on the bottom of the page. You may want to review the example of Kathy on page 63.
- When you have finished, check out your plan with a friend. Are there any steps that you left out? Are time estimates realistic?

. . . more on Column 3 later . . .

IMPLEMENTATION PLAN

Action to be Taken	Estimated Time	Reward

Time Line for Implementation Plan

Months											
1	2	3	4	5	6	7	8	9	10	11	12

MAINTAINING MOTIVATION

Two problems frequently encountered by people implementing career decisions are an unclear plan and failure to follow through. We have just considered a method for developing clear plans for implementing career decisions. Let's now consider a procedure for helping you maintain motivation to follow your plan.

Many tasks involved in implementing career decisions have no immediate reward or payoff. For example, writing a resume, researching employers, and attending a job interview workshop may seem only vaguely related to obtaining a specific position. Because of the lack of immediate rewards, many people encounter difficulty in maintaining adequate motivation to complete the steps in their implementation plan. One way to deal with the motivation problem is to build interim rewards into your plan.

The concept of reward involves choosing a pleasant experience and rewarding yourself with it after you have performed each desired task. For example, you might reward yourself for completing a term paper by going skiing, taking a bike ride, visiting friends, or going out to dinner. Planning such rewards can help you stay with your plan until it has been completed.

To build rewards into your implementation plan select a pleasant activity or experience for each task in the plan. The activities and experiences are your rewards. They should be easily accessible and applied soon after a task has been done.

Following is an example of how you might build rewards into a career implementation plan:

ACTION TO BE TAKEN	ESTIMATED TIME	REWARD
Select five potential employers	2 weeks	Play tennis
Research each employer	2 weeks	Go to movie with friend
Complete a resume	2 weeks	Have coffee with friend
Sharpen interview skills	1 week	Go canoeing

To practice identifying your own rewards try the following.

First, list below ten activities or rewards which you enjoy and which are easily accessible.

1.	6.
2.	7.
3.	8.
4.	9.
5.	10.

Next, review your implementation plan on page 65. Select one of the rewards you have just listed for each task in your plan and enter these in the last column.

Finally, if you think you may still have trouble staying on target, enlist the help of a friend. Arrange to talk with this person frequently to review what you've done as a means of following through. For added incentive you can build your rewards around activities that involve spending time with this person.

LEISURE
7

- *The purpose of this section is to define your leisure desires and select activities which meet these desires.*

In the first section, career was defined as consisting of job, vocation, and leisure activities. In this section we will examine the notion of leisure and describe how you can increase satisfaction in that part of your career. Perhaps your first reaction to this idea is, "Who needs help in enjoying their leisure time? My problem is getting the time." Getting leisure time is a real concern for many busy students. There are only 24 hours in a day and many of us use 20-22 of those hours attending class, working, studying, sleeping, and caring for ourselves and others.

Whatever amount of leisure time you have, using it purposefully is important. Good leisure doesn't just happen. Similar to most things in life, taking the time to think and plan usually brings better results. "But shouldn't leisure be spontaneous," you may be thinking. Perhaps, but consider the results of "spontaneous" leisure. The weekend you eagerly anticipated, but turned out to be a bore because all of your friends left town; the disappointing evening when the theater was sold out; the lost afternoon when you couldn't get a tennis court; making five phone calls at 6:00 p.m. Friday only to discover everyone had other plans.

These kinds of leisure disappointments need not happen. You can have enjoyable leisure if you take some time for self-assessment and planning. The first step to improving your leisure is to clarify your desires. What kinds of satisfactions do you want from your leisure activities?

While we all have a variety of desires at any point in our lives, we are not always fully aware of them. Below are 15 desires which people give as reasons for engaging in leisure activities. As a means of clarifying your leisure desires, read the list and indicate how important each desire is to you by making a check mark (✓) in the appropriate column.

Desires	Very Strong	Medium Strong	So-So or Less
– **Desire to Meet Other People.** A leisure activity can be a way to meet other people. If your day is filled with books, lectures, independent study, and other students, you might desire a leisure activity in which you can meet new and different people.			
– **Desire to Extend the Pocketbook.** A look at your monthly budget necessitates considering leisure activities which help it S-T-R-E-T-C-H. Gardening, sewing, and furniture making are budget-saving leisure activities.			
– **Desire to Increase Pleasant Family Interaction.** "The family that plays together stays together." Many families choose leisure activities that will assist in strengthening family relationships.			

Desires	Very Strong	Medium Strong	So-So or Less
– **Desire to be Alone.** If people interruptions and hassles abound in your daily existence, the desire to be alone can be the main reason for selecting leisure activities. If this is your goal, the actual activity is not as important as the guarantee that the time spent will be private.	✓		
– **Desire to Produce a Product.** To some extent we all like to "see results." If you are not producing anything notable or worthy, you might want to start weaving, refinishing antiques, carving, painting, or something else you can point to and say, "See, I did that."		✓	
– **Desire to Use Intellect, Talent, or Feel Creative.** Similarly, many people have talents for which they will never be paid, but which can be pursued at leisure. The advantages to using musical, artistic, dramatic, and intellectual talents on an amateur basis is that you, not an employer, control the activity.	✓		
– **Desire to Help Others.** We usually feel better about ourselves, and the world in general, when we help others. The desire to help can be satisfied by a great variety of activities. These include direct service help, such as volunteering in a hospital or social agency, working in student government and staffing a political campaign.		✓	
– **Desire to be Different.** We all like to believe we're unique. If life seems routine, you might want a dramatic or at least a different type of free time activity. A female race driver, a male doing needlepoint, or anyone becoming involved in a risky or adventurous activity would be examples of being different.	✓		
– **Desire to Exercise.** Passing a certain birthday or getting a good look in the mirror makes many of us seek exercise. A common problem is finding a form of exercise which is also satisfying. Combining this desire with another (e.g., desire for companionship) is one solution.	✓		

Desires	Very Strong	Medium Strong	So-So or Less
– **Desire for Companionship.** Sharing time in an activity with a friend or loved one is very desirable. Oftentimes we don't care so much what the activity is as long as we can share the experience with the other person.			
– **Desire to Compete.** We all enjoy competing at times. Competition can be against another person, in the context of teams, or even with yourself. Leisure activities can provide the excitement of competition without the risks one might face in other areas of your life.			
– **Desire to Appreciate Nature.** Nature and the rewards it can offer in peace, solitude, and scientific wonder are hard to match. Responding to the call of the wild can bring a better balance to life.			
– **Desire to Escape.** There are times when escape from unpleasant or boring reality is our paramount desire. A stressful relationship, a high-pressure student role, or the harassment of parenting are examples of situations in which escape to some frivolous activity may be the most beneficial use of leisure.			
– **Desire for Aesthetic Enrichment.** As people come to appreciate art, music, drama, and other cultural experiences, the desire for aesthetic enrichment grows. The satisfaction derived is a very personal experience and one highly valued by some people.			
– **Desire to be Entertained.** Not as lofty as the prior desires, but a real desire by most of us. Activities such as watching a movie, listening to a bluegrass group, or spending an evening watching TV fulfill the desire of entertainment with minimal personal commitment.			

Now look at your check marks. What have you discovered about yourself? What are the strongest desires in your leisure profile? What desires are not expecially important? How much did you base your responses on experience? Wishful thinking? How much on assumptions? Many people discover that there are certain conditions attached to their desires. Joan, for example, often stated the desire to be alone, to have a lot of private time in her leisure. When asked to examine this desire, she discovered an important underlying condition was always having the option of being with people. Think also about your changing self. Have you emphasized current desires, or those you had before coming to college?

Now let's turn your desires into potential leisure activities. Review the chart you just completed and select your three strongest desires. Write them in the boxes below.

Important Leisure Desires

DESIRE 1	DESIRE 2	DESIRE 3

Next list activities that are interesting to you that meet each of the desires. At this point don't consider such realities as time, money, skill or energy. Just be concerned with listing interesting activities. If you get stuck, look for some ideas by talking with a friend or browsing through a magazine or newspaper.

As an example, look at the lists of a student who selected these three activities.

DESIRE TO BE ALONE	DESIRE FOR COMPANIONSHIP	DESIRE TO FEEL CREATIVE
Bicycling	Card Games	Make Own Patterns
Jogging	Board Games	Design Rya Rugs
Jigsaw Puzzles	Group Reading	Decorate Room
Nature Walks	Watching TV and Discussion	Photography
Bird Watching	Movies	Ceramics
Reading	Circus/Rodeo/Carnivals/Parks	Ethnic Cooking
Photography	Camping	Indoor Gardening
Painting	Stamp Collections	Growing Flowers
Gardening	Boating	Write a Story
Beachcombing	Building Model Kits	Design Furniture
Making Models	Bicycling	Plan a Trip
Word Puzzles	Table Tennis	Paint
Cooking	Horseback Riding	
Fishing	Cooking	
Woodworking	Taking Pictures Together	
Hiking		

Now for the test of reality. For any activity to meet its maximum potential, you must be able to meet the requirements of that activity. You have made three lists of activities that meet three current desires. Next we will consider whether or not you have the resources to meet the requirements for a particular activity.

Look at your three lists of activities and select one activity that is very appealing to you. Write it here. [ ] Now let's consider that activity in terms of the following conditions. First describe the requirements for each condition by noting the answer to each of the questions. Then check (✓) those requirements you can meet—or are willing to meet.

CONDITIONS	REQUIREMENTS	CAN MEET (✓)
TIME—How many hours weekly or monthly, or if more appropriate, seasonally, does the activity take? Could this activity fit into your schedule?		
MONEY—How much initial investment as well as ongoing costs are involved? Could these expenses fit into your budget?		
SPACE—How much physical space does your activity require, e.g., a place to put your sewing machine or shop tools? Can you meet the minimal requirements?		
APPTITUDE, TRAINING, AND SKILLS—What aptitude or skills does your training require? If you do not possess these, can they be acquired?		
EFFECT OF ACTIVITY ON OTHERS—Who will be affected? Can you cope with other's reactions to your new interest?		

Did the activity pass the reality text? Can you (or are you willing) to meet the requirements for this activity? If so, you probably have a good chance of gaining satisfaction from it. If not, pick other activities on your list and apply the reality test until you find one which passes.

If beginning the activity seems difficult, here are a few tips for getting started. If equipment is required, you may not have to purchase it initially. Most recreational gear can be rented, as can items such as cameras and bicycles. Community colleges and park departments offer courses on a wide variety of leisure activities as well as maintain facilities such as courts, darkrooms, woodshops, looms, and other craft facilities. If you do buy equipment, find a seller who is knowledgeable and *interested* in helping you get off to a good start. Talking with people who are already into your new activity is another way to quickly broaden your information base.

In general, take a few minutes to think through what will be involved in the activity, problems or frustrations you might encounter, and how you might deal with them. Finally, learn from your new experience. Is it satisfying? If not, why? What did you learn about your leisure desires from the experience and how can you use this insight in selecting other leisure activities?

CAREER INFORMATION
8

Implementing career plans and decisions often requires various kinds of information. This section is an annotated list of information sources. The books and directories included hardly scratch the surface of the vast amount of information available. The resources included have been found to be particularly helpful to people in periods of career transition. The following categories are used.

- Educational Opportunities and Plans
  - Four-Year Colleges and Universities
    - General Information
    - College Admissions Testing
  - Occupational Education
  - Two-Year Colleges and Schools
- Financial (This list is included because most career decisions have financial implications.)
- Leisure
- Marriage (This selected annotated list is included because many college graduates are facing this decision.)
- Occupational Plans and Opportunities
  - Career Planning
  - International
  - Job Hunting
  - Researching Aids
  - Women

As we hope you realize, none of the books contain the answer. They do however contain facts, ideas, and descriptions which should be useful as you proceed with the process of making your own career decisions and plans.

Perhaps 75% of the books described are relatively inexpensive paperbacks. Books which are library references are indicated by an asterisk (*) preceding the bibliographic reference.

EDUCATIONAL OPPORTUNITIES AND PLANS

Four Year Colleges and Universities

General Information

**The College Blue Book*, latest edition. New York: CCM Information Corporation. (Probably the most comprehensive and detailed educational directory available.) It consists of 10 volumes. The contents of several volumes are summarized below. The summaries are excerpted from Volume 1.

Volume 1: *Guide and Index to College Blue Book*

Special Lists of Colleges
This section includes lists of Colleges Accepting "C" students; Predominantly Black Colleges; Women's Colleges; Men's Colleges; Two-Year Colleges; and Colleges Offering ROTC. Analytical Index to All Volumes of CBB, in Alphabetical Order.

Volume 2: *U.S. Colleges: Tabular Data*

Volume 3: *U.S. Colleges: Narrative Descriptions*
Each of the 3,400 colleges listed in Volume 2 is fully described in Volume 3. Exact procedures are given for filing admission applications, and campus facilities are discussed.

Volume 4: *Degrees Offered, by Subject*

Volume 5: *Degrees Offered, by College*

Volume 6: *College Atlas*
This volume describes the geographical location of each of the schools listed in Volumes 2 and 3. Airline routes, bus and train schedules, as well as highway information, are given for each town. In addition, a full-page map of each state identifies the location of all colleges within the state.

Volume 7: *Specialized Educational Programs*
This volume offers information about many educational opportunities available in the U.S. and abroad. Associated institutions of Higher Education are listed and described; complete information on church-related colleges and universities is given; general information regarding accredited schools and courses offered through the National Home Study Council is given; and correspondence courses offered by institutions that are affiliated with the National University Extension Association are listed.

In a separate section called "Study Abroad," there is complete information about enrollment, curricula, and tuition for most of the major universities abroad.

Volume 8: *Professions, Careers, and Accreditation*
The first section of this volume, *Choosing a Career*, defines and identifies professions and careers likely to be of greatest interest to *College Blue Book* users. Accreditation Associations are listed, together with the schools that are accredited by each organization. In addition, Professional and Educational Associations related to the professions listed earlier in the volume, are listed and described.

Volume 9: *Scholarships, Fellowships, and Grants*
This volume lists over $100,000,000 in available scholarships.

Volume 10: *Secondary Schools in the U.S.*

**The College Handbook*, current edition. New York: College Entrance Examination Board. Describes each of the colleges which are affiliated with College Entrance Examination Board. Written to the potential student with his questions in mind.

College Admissions Testing

American College Testing Program
College Entrance Examination Board

Many colleges require students to take the examinations of one of these organizations as part of their admission procedure. The tests are given several times each year on specified dates. School counselors have the testing schedules and application materials for both programs.

Occupational Education

*Miller, A.E. and Brown, B.I. *National Directory of Schools and Vocations.* State School Publications, No. Springfield, Pa., 1967.

Lists colleges according to occupational programs from "accountant to X-Ray clerk." An initial reference, little descriptive information.

*Russell, Max W., Ed., *The Blue Book of Occupational Education.* New York: CCM Corp., 1971.

Presents information on nearly 12,000 occupational schools in the United States. Describes schools and indexes by programs of instruction offered from accounting to zinc plate making. The main headings from the table of contents suggest the scope of the book. These are:

Occupational Schools of the United States
Curricula and Programs of Instruction
Accredited Business Schools
Two-Year Institutions of the United States
Accredited Home Study Schools
Schools Offering Two-Year Library Technology Programs
Accredited Medical and Dental Technological Schools of the United States
Nursing Schools of the United States
Schools Approved for Veteran's Training
Apprenticeship Training
United States Occupational Training Programs
Guide to Nation's Job Openings
Occupational Descriptions
Financial Aid
Sources of Additional Information

Two-Year Colleges and Schools

*Campbell, Gordon, *Community Colleges in Canada.* Toronto/New York/London: Ryerson Press, 1971.

Brief descriptions of Canadian community colleges listed by province. Includes academic, financial, and admission information.

*Cass, James and Bernbaum, *Comparative Guide to Two-Year Colleges and Four-Year Specialized Schools and Programs.* Harper and Row, 1969.

Brief listing of many community colleges. Special value is its emphasis on colleges offering programs in the performing arts, including: art, dance, music, theater, radio-t.v., and film.

*Gleazer, Edmond J., (Ed), *American Junior Colleges*, 8th edition. American Council on Education.

Sponsored by the American Council on Education and the American Association of Junior Colleges, this volume describes all two-year institutions accredited by nationally recognized accrediting agencies. Covers all states and territories and lists public and private institutions separately. Provides both academic and financial information. There is also a listing of two-year institutions according to the programs offered in various occupational fields.

FINANCIAL

Callenbach, Ernest. *Living Poor With Style.* New, New York: Bantam Books, 1972. $1.95.

For those who want advice on saving money *Living Poor With Style* is a must. There are a multitude of suggestions regarding expenditures for food, shelter, transportation, furnishings, clothing, medical services, recreation, education and training, and raising children. The advice is laced with comments about governmental policy and social issues. There is a definite bias: it is "in" to be poor and against the mainstream culture. Aware of this, readers can objectively read the ideas and useful hints and judge whether or not they can use them in their lifestyle preference.

Crook De Camp, Catherine. *The Money Tree.* New York: New American Library, 1972.

This book is useful for those who need general information in many financial areas. After reading the book, one inexperienced in money matters should feel they have a little better grasp of how to proceed with financial decisions.

The book begins with an elementary discussion of assets and liabilities, and suggestions for developing a spending plan. Comparative government data on family spending are given. Methods for the art and discipline of record keeping are discussed and illustrative forms are displayed in the appendix.

Helpful chapters are included on credit buying, building or buying/renting a home; buying a car; and financing a car. In each of these chapters specific information is given regarding whom to see, what to look for, and what to compare. Other chapters are included on shopping skills and common fraudulent business practices.

The author also deals with the issues of saving, stocks, and social security. The appendix includes a good bibliography for various financial issues.

Ferguson, Marilyn and Mike. *Champagne Living on a Beer Budget.* New York: Berkeley Publishing Company, 1973. $1.95.

The usual topics of consuming or spending wisely in the areas of food, housing, furnishings, clothing, transportation, babies, medicine, gift-giving, recreation and travel, and governmental benefits are treated. Other topics, not usually treated in similar books, include how to: save on telephone rates, state a consumer complaint, invest money, rent almost anything, and plan efficiently.

The writing style of this book makes it particularly interesting and useful. Each chapter includes a series of anecdotes and specific suggestions or techniques. Almost every page includes a useful suggestion for saving money.

Halcomb, Ruth. *Money and The Working Ms.* Chatsworth, California: Books for Better Living, 1974. $1.25.

This book is designed to assist the single working woman do effective financial planning. The author, a single working mother, states that the book's purpose is "to help you initiate a total program for wise spending and saving."

After describing case studies of ineffective women spenders, the next few chapters urge the reader to make a master plan complete with goals and a careful study of one's assets and liabilities. The next step is to develop a workable budget. The items of most budgets—food, shelter, furnishings, clothes, entertainment, transportation—are specifically discussed in subsequent chapters, and guidelines are presented for determining the priorities within.

Other financial concerns such as dealing with emergencies and taxes are also discussed. A special chapter discusses economic and psychological problems in raising children alone. The book concludes with a brief discussion of investment possibilities for the single woman.

The Mother Earth News Almanac. New York: Bantam Books, 1973. $1.95.

All those interested in a book chock-full of ideas and helpful hints from A to Z will enjoy *The Mother Earth News Almanac.* This 361-page almanac has literally thousands of practical suggestions and how-to information. These include ideas which are:

Practical (how to make compost)
Fun (building a kite)
Old-timey (folk medicine)
Designed for those wanting to get "back to the land" (tips on raising animals)
Helpful in improving city and suburban life (how to grow a sprout garden in a closet)
Futuristic (using solar energy for heating homes)

A number of the ideas enumerated can save the reader money. A good book for a rainy afternoon, and one you will use as a ready reference thereafter.

Poriss, Martin. *How to Live Cheap But Good.* New York, New York: Dell Publishing Co., Inc., 1971. $1.50.

This book is primarily geared to the apartment dweller and college student but because of the variety and clarity of money-saving hints it is recommended for others as well. The six chapters include the following:

Home Is Where You Find It
—Includes hints on how to find and select the best living unit for you.
—Deals with signing a lease.
—Has apartment hunter's check list.

A Moving Experience
—Includes a step-by-step procedure of moving your possessions.

Shoveling Out, Fixing Up and Furnishing
—Specific advice on cleaning and fixing one's home and furnishings.

Thought for Food
—Information ranges from what kind of equipment should be in the kitchen, to how one should buy fruits and vegetables, to cooking methods and techniques.

Getting Your Money's Worth
—Includes ideas for saving on clothes, health care, and utility bills as well as how to be an effective consumer.

Home Repairs for the Poet
—Step-by-step procedures for repairing plumbing, electrical fixtures, doors, windows, and radiators.

Overall a very useful book.

Scaduto, Anthony. *Getting the Most for Your Money.* New York: Paperback Library, 1970. $ .95.

A real gem for general consumer information—such as skills for wise shopping and charts showing which months different items (e.g., appliances, clothing, cars, etc.) are most likely to be on sale. The book deals in depth with major spending items. Chapters are included on:

—Buying food
—Buying clothes
—Household appliance purchases
—Buying and maintaining a car
—Recreational spending
—Financing college educations
—Buying properties and life insurance
—Medical expenses

Each chapter provides specific facts, information, or shopping hints for making the most of your dollar. (For example, the chapter on buying food provides general food buying hints and specific buying tips for meat, dairy products, baked goods, etc.)

The chapter on financing a college education asks the reader to complete a worksheet estimating and comparing expenses at the different colleges being considered, and then describes the financial options available (student employment, loans, scholarships, and grants) and lists where to write for more information.

Shortney, Joan Ranson. *How to Live on Nothing.* New York, New York: Pocket Books, 1973. $ .95.

Highly recommended by *The Whole Earth Catalogue* for its practical and accurate information, this 320-page book suggests how to save money on the following topics: food, clothing, household furnishings, buying a house, maintenance and repair work, heating your house, gift-giving, vacationing, medicine, and knowing your social benefits. Information is thorough on each topic, and the reader is usually provided instructions for researching the topics discussed. Sometimes the reader is provided an inexpensive source of further information, such as a governmental publication.

The last chapter of the book consists of a list of 100 usually discarded objects, and ways to re-use them. The good life, suggests the author, can be found by using the skills found in this book.

LEISURE

Lowery, Lucie. *Your Leisure Time . . . How to Enjoy It.* Los Angeles: Ward Richie Press, 1972. $1.95.

Intended for those who live in the Los Angeles area, the book is still a useful guide for those living in other geographical areas. Following a brief discussion of the current status of leisure time, are seven chapters on various areas of leisure. Topics include high-risk leisure pursuits, artistic pursuits, scientific hobbies, physical activities, intellectual activities, volunteer activities, and off-beat leisure activities. Each chapter is punctuated with interesting stories about people that engage in the leisure activities discussed.

A "fun test" gives the reader his "leisure quotient." The book concludes with a list of people and organizations in the Los Angeles area that can assist in fulfilling one's leisure needs.

*Overs, Robert; O'Connor, Elizabeth; DeMarco, Barbara. *Guide to Avocational Activities.* Milwaukee, Wisconsin: Curative Workshop of Milwaukee, 1972.

This is a three-volume study which has provided a classification system for leisure activities. The system uses the following nine categories:

Games
Sports
Nature Activities
Collection Activities
Craft Activities
Art and Music Activities
Education, Entertainment, and Cultural Activities
Volunteer Activities
Organizational Activities

There are literally hundreds of activities briefly described in the three volumes. In addition to the description, each activity is rated according to environmental, social-psychological, and cost factors. Of special interest to some readers is an indication of the extent to which various kinds of physical impairments limit doing each activity.

MARRIAGE

Bach, George R. and Deutsch, Ronald M. *Pairing: How to Achieve Genuine Intimacy.* New York: Avon Books, 1970. $1.25.

Dr. Bach, the author of *The Intimate Enemy*, has essentially outlined the same type of techniques as in his first book. The techniques, developed and used at The Institute of Group Psychotherapy, rely heavily on the expression of feelings in the here-and-now. Some of the technique may appear rather "gimmicky." There are several useful suggestions and guidelines for effective communication procedures. The authors have coined many words to describe "bad" nonintimate behaviors (gunny-sacking, mind-raping, thinging) and "correct" intimate behaviors (leveling, meditation) which at times detract from the instructive value of the book because one is "caught up" in lingo. The book does succeed in demonstrating that we often misread an intimate and that the use of some fairly basic communication procedures can produce mutually satisfying results.

Bernard, Jessie. *The Future of Marriage.* New York, New York: A Bantam Book, 1972. $1.95.

A very readable, but academic view of the past, present, and future of marriage. The author, a sociologist, has written a number of other books including *The Sex Game* and *The Academic Woman.*

When discussing the future of marriage it is important to state whose marriage is being discussed; the husband's or the wife's. Considerable research shows that there are, in fact, two marriages in each union, and they often do not coincide.

After an interesting discussion of the history and current status of marriage, the author presents some other male and female writers' options for the future of marriage. These range from celibacy to communal neighborhoods. The author's own view is that marriage does have a future—a future of many options. These options will create many new demands, but the author does not state that the marriage partners will be happier or better adjusted than currently. She ends by making a plea to upgrade the wife's marriage.

Lederer, William J. and Jackson, Don D. *The Mirages of Marriage.* New York: W.W. Norton and Company, Inc., 1968. $10.

The Mirages of Marriage talks about marriage as it is, not as the romantics would idealize it. After a brief description of the history of marriage, many of the false assumptions of modern marriage are identified. For example, the authors state that one false assumption is that loneliness will be cured by marriage.

Marriage is described as an interlocking system. The behavior of one spouse creates a reaction from the other spouse. At many times the behavior of one spouse conflicts with what the other desires (e.g., disagreement on which T.V. show to watch, where to go on a vacation, or how to spend a bonus). Specific techniques and exercises to train couples to negotiate are outlined.

The book also contains a marital check list and a discussion on the use of marital counselors.

O'Neill, Nena and O'Neill, George. *Open Marriage.* New York: Avon Books, 1973. $1.95.

According to the authors "open marriage means an honest and open relationship between two people, based on the equal freedom and identity of both partners. It involves a verbal, intellectual and emotional commitment to the right of each to grow as an individual within the marriage." The O'Neills identify eight cardinal guidelines to achieving an open marriage. These are:

1. Living for Now and Realistic Expectations
2. Privacy
3. Open and Honest Communication
4. Flexibility in Roles
5. Open Companionship
6. Equality
7. Identity
8. Trust

The core of the book outlines methods for following the guidelines. The O'Neills contend that achieving an open marriage is a "self-reinforcing, regenerative, and growth-enhancing system" that continues to expand.

OCCUPATIONAL PLANS AND OPPORTUNITIES

Career Planning

Beitz, Charles and Washburn, Michael. *Creating the Future.* New York: Bantam Books, 1974. $1.95.

Subtitled "A Guide to Living and Working for Social Change," the book is a very useful resource for those with such aspirations. The author claims that people can work for social change both within established institutions or through creating alternative institutions. An introductory section describes idealized communities in terms of services and governmental operations. Major concern is with specific areas of social change and how to find out more about these areas. Included are chapters on media, education, health, business, politics, science and technology, church, labor, and the federal government. Each chapter outlines social change possibilities and concludes with extensive resource lists of people, places, or things to contact for further information. If social change is your thing, this is a good buy!

Dictionary of Occupations Titles, Volume 1, *Definitions of Titles*. Washington, D.C.: U.S. Government Printing Office, 1965.

Volume 1 of the *Dictionary of Occupations Titles* has definitions of 35,500 job titles arranged alphabetically. The definitions are short (10-15 lines), and specific about job duties and responsibilities. The basic reference in occupational information.

*Forrester, Gertrude. *Occupational Literature: An Annotated Bibliography*. New York, New York: The H.W. Wilson Company, 1971. $15.00.

A reference book to use in your local library for finding sources of information on specific occupations. Most of this 600-page volume is an annotated bibliography of books and pamphlets describing occupations. Occupations are listed alphabetically starting with Able Seaman and ending with Zoologist. Under Zoologist, for example, ten books and pamphlets are listed (prices included). Addresses of all publishers listed are included.

Various specialized bibliographies include: job seeking, occupations for the handicapped, planning a career, scholarships, professional counseling services, apprenticeships, and foreign study and employment.

The Graduate. Knoxville, Tennessee: Approach 13-30 Corporation, 1973. $2.

An annual magazine for graduating college seniors subtitled "A Handbook for Leaving School." Using the style and format of newstand publications, the brochure has more visual appeal than many other publications dealing with similar information. To order, send $2.00 to Approach 13-30 Corporation, 1005 Maryville Pike SW, Knoxville, Tennessee 37920.

Articles range in topics from job outlooks to issues faced by minority graduates to a special section on "The Real World Catalog." The latter section covers such items as arranging your finances, insurance, costs of moving, buying a stereo, and other "real world" facts. A helpful publication for the recent graduate.

McKee, Bill. *New Careers for Teachers*. Chicago, Illinois: Henry Regnery Company, 1972. $4.95.

For a variety of reasons fewer positions are currently available for teachers. This book is intended to assist teachers find positions in teaching and non-teaching fields. The publication is divided into four sections:

I—A self-evaluation of interests, aptitudes, experience and knowledge
II—Descriptions of jobs for which little or no re-training would be necessary
III—The nitty gritty of getting a job—resumes and interviews
IV—Nontraditional careers in education

A good place to start for teachers who find they must (or want to) make a career change.

Occupational Outlook Handbook. U.S. Government Printing Office. Published bi-annually. $6.25.

A reference available in most public libraries. More than 800 occupations are discussed in the *Handbook*. Each individual occupational listing, usually 2-3 pages, describes the nature of the work, places of employment, training, other qualifications, advancement opportunities, employment outlook, earnings, and working conditions. Places to write for additional information are included at the end of each description. This reference is useful for all educational and age levels.

Splaver, Sarah. *Nontraditional College Routes to Careers.* New York: Julian Messner, 1975 .
A helpful listing of the new, nontraditional college education programs. It includes brief, but specific, information on correspondence study, study abroad, cooperative education, multimedia learning, nontraditional degree programs, and other innovations. The result to the reader should be that higher education is attainable and FUN.

*Teal, Everett A. *The Occupational Thesaurus* (2 Vol.) Bethlehem, Pennsylvania: Lehigh University, 1971. $11.95 for the set.
This reference set is designed to assist the reader to learn the job opportunities which exist for particular college majors. The following college majors are included: anthropology, economics, history, languages, mathematics, political science, psychology, sociology, accounting, biology, chemistry, finance, geology, management, marketing, physics, and transportation.

Entry occupations are listed for each of these major fields of study. The effect, particularly for the reader in liberal arts, is the realization that many options are available for those with undergraduate degrees.

**Vocational Biographies.* Sauk Centre, Minnesota: Vocational Biographies, 1972.
The *Vocational Biographies* series is a helpful tool in career planning. Each series contains 6 volumes, and each volume has 25 4-page case histories describing the careers of people in the vocations spotlighted. Biographies conclude with specific job facts and places to write for further information.

The strength of *Vocational Biographies* is that information is presented in an interesting, involving manner. Blue collar as well as white collar occupations are included.

Vocational Guidance Manuals, 620 South Fifth Street, Louisville, Kentucky 40202.
This publisher produces a series of books about specific vocational fields. Each book describes in detail current realities in the field. Titles include:

Opportunities in Forestry Careers
Opportunities in Environmental Careers
Opportunities in Publishing
Opportunities in Foreign Language Careers
Opportunities in Technical Writing Today
Opportunities in Graphic Communications
Opportunities in Carpentry Careers

A complete catalog of VGM books is available on request at no charge.

Weaver, Peter. *You, Inc.: A Detailed Escape Route to Being Your Own Boss.* Garden City, New York: Dolphin Books, 1973.
The author started his own business after working 20 years for "the establishment." His book outlines the pitfalls but stresses the advantages of being on your own. The book combines how-to-do-it with interesting stories of those who have. A good place to start if you want your own ideas and creativity to guide your life.

International

*Angel, Juvenal L. *Dictionary of American Firms Operating in Foreign Countries.* World Trade Academy Press, 1971.
Includes data on more than 3,000 American corporations operating overseas. Arranged alphabetically with cross references both by geography and product. If you want to work overseas for a business, this source is the place to start.

*Calvert, Robert. *A Definitive Study of Your Future in International Service.* Richard Rosen Press, 1969.

Contains a discussion of careers with religious, voluntary, and governmental organizations overseas. There is also a chapter on teaching opportunities abroad.

Hopkins, Robert. *I've Had It.* New York: Holt, Rinehart, and Winston, 1972.

Subtitled "A Practical Guide to Moving Abroad," the book discusses the problems and advantages of moving abroad. The author relates the cycles that some people might experience if they actually make such a move. These include an initial period of elation, followed by a period of despondency and considering moving back to the U.S. and finally a period of leveling off when one realistically realizes the disadvantages and advantages in one's chosen environment. Information is included on job availability, taxes, climate, schools, and language training. Also included are lists of sources of books, pamphlets, and guides.

**International Yellow Pages.* New York: Reuben H. Donnelley Corp., $20.

Lists business and professional firms and individuals from 150 countries throughout the world under headings which are descriptive of the products and services they have to offer in world-wide trade. English, French, German, and Spanish language versions. Divided into six geographical areas: Africa, Asia, Australia and Oceania, Europe, Latin America, Caribbean, North America. Lists businesses and organizations of an international character.

Job Hunting

Bolles, Richard Nelson. *What Color is Your Parachute?* Berkeley, California: Ten Speed Press, 1973. $3.95.

Subtitled, "A Practical Manual for Job-Hunters & Career Changers," the book begins by describing why traditional strategies for job search are ineffective. The author discourages what he calls "the numbers game" approach to job hunting (e.g., sending out 100 resumes to get six job interviews).

Bolles' 3-step prescription for job search consists of:

"1. Deciding 'just exactly what you want to do.'

"2. Deciding 'just exactly where you want to do it, through your own research and personal survey.'

"3. Researching the organizations that interest you at great length, and then approaching the one individual in each organization who has the power to hire you for the job that you have decided you want to do."

The remainder of the book describes exactly how to complete these three steps. This is one of the better how-to books on job searching.

Chamberlain, Betty. *The Artist's Guide to His Market.* New York: Watson-Guptill Publications, 1975.

If you are an artist who has passed the rank of amateur, this is your book. It describes the ins and outs of working with a gallery, contractual agreements, pricing your work, publicity, and many other practical areas of concern to the self-employed artist.

Haldane, Bernard; Haldane, Jean and Martin, Lowell. *Job Power Now: The Young People's Job Finding Guide.* Washington, D. C.: Acopolis Books, Ltd., 1976.

An excellent book for the younger job hunter. It assists the reader to analyze the skills he has accumulated in all aspects of his life and assists him in presenting this information to the potential employer.

Irish, Richard K. *Go Hire Yourself an Employer.* Garden City, New York: Anchor Books, 1973. $2.95.

A question and answer format is used in this how-to-do-a-job-search book. Traditional strategies of completing resumes and setting goals are covered. The author also makes the point that you, the employee, are really hiring an employer and thus it is up to you to interview the interviewer and negotiate your salary. Outlines for implementing this strategy are presented.

The last two chapters of the book deal with special employment situations (being a CO, a woman, a minority, handicapped) and opportunities with the federal government.

Jacquish, Michael P. *Personal Resumé Preparation.* New York: John Wiley and Sons, Inc., 1968.

An excellent guide for resumé preparation. The case for an effective resumé is made clearly. Four resumé formats are clearly discussed and illustrated (chronological, functional, organizational, and creative). The reader is helped to assess which is best for his/her particular situation. Several suggestions are given for dealing with sometimes 'sticky' issues, such as, reason for leaving last position, age, desired salary, and marital status. Clear, concise information and illustrations are given on such considerations as the actual typing, paper, and printing specifications for the resumé. The last chapter details guidelines to use when writing cover letters. Examples of cover letters are included.

Larson, Darold E. *How to Find a Job.* New York: Ace Books, 1974. $1.95.

Well organized book on the art of job hunting. A good beginning book when faced with a job finding problem.

Nutter, Carolyn F. *The Resumé Workbook.* Cranston, R.I.: Carroll Press, 1970. $3.50.

As the title indicates, the approach of this how-to book is in workbook format. The introduction section describes and illustrates four kinds of resumés which are the chronological, analytical, functional, and imaginative approaches. The next section of the workbook illustrates what resumé might be most appropriate for a specific job-hunting situation, such as mature woman, graduating college senior, military retiree, and high school graduate.

Research Aids

*Colgate, Craig, Editor. *1976 National Trade and Professional Associations of the United States and Canada and Labor Unions.* Washington, D. C.: Columbia Books, Inc., annual.

This directory lists 5700 organizations. A very good job searching and career planning aid because it indexes the organizations alphabetically, geographically, by name of executives in the corporation, by amount of budget the organization has, and by the type of product or field with which the organization is concerned.

**College Placement Annual.* Bethlehem, Penn.: College Placement Council, Inc. Published annually. $5.00

This reference is available at college placement offices as well as many public libraries. One of the most useful tools for any college graduate seeking employment, the *Annual* contains information on United States employers that hire college graduates. Information given on each employer includes the following: brief description of the nature of the business or organization, name of the college recruiting officer, number of employees, and occupational openings for which the organization will recruit. The *Annual* is indexed by academic disciplines and geographical areas.

**Directory of Public Service Internships: Opportunities for the Graduate, Post Graduate, and Mid-Career Professional.* Washington, D. C.: National Center for Public Service Internship Programs: $6.00.

This directory, which intends to revise yearly, is a listing of public service agency programs designed for the post-college grad. A one- or two-page program description outlines and describes admission requirements.

**Encyclopedia of Associations.* Vol. I: *National Organizations of the U.S.* Detroit: Gale Research Co., 1970.

A comprehensive list of all types of national associations arranged by broad classification, and with an alphabetical and key-word index. Gives names of chief officer, brief statements of activities, number of members, names of publications, etc. National associations can often give useful career planning information as well as specific help in a job search.

**Encyclopedia of Business Information Sources.* (2 vols.) Detroit, Michigan: Gale Research Co., 1970.

This two-volume encyclopedia is a good beginning source to use to find out where to seek further information on a business topic. The first volume is arranged alphabetically and the topics range from abrasives industry to zoological gardens. Under each topic specific statistical sources, price sources, handbooks and manuals, periodicals, and trade associations are listed for further information. The contents in Volume II are for those interested in international business information, and the contents are arranged by geographical location from Africa to Zanzibar.

**Federal Career Directory: A Guide for College Students.* Washington, D.C.: United States Civil Service Commission, 1973.

If you want to consider the federal government as an employer and you have an undergraduate college degree, start with this publication. It should be available in your local library or in any college placement office. The *Directory* is divided into three parts:

Part I—Description of federal career occupations
Part II—Description of federal agencies
Part III—Job briefs listed by college major

Read this before taking the Federal Service Entrance Examination. For those who have a graduate degree contact your regional Federal Job Information Center and ask for information about mid-level positions in your area of specialty. Those with a community college degree or high school diploma should contact the Information Center for publications relevant to your background and experience.

Greenfield, Phyllis O. *Educator's Placement Guide.* National Center for Information on Careers in Education, 1972.

This small guide gives a wealth of information, including:

—Current trends in educational staffing needs
—Addresses for certification information by state
—Services of state education associations
—Services of professional and private agencies
—Addresses of independent, federal, international, and innovative schools
—Information on non-teaching careers (e.g., educational publishing houses, regional educational labs, research centers)
—Sample application letters and resumés.

**Industrial Research Laboratories of the United States.* National Research Council. Published yearly.

Contains information on 5,237 non-governmental laboratories devoted to fundamental and applied research, and operated by 3,115 organizations, mostly industrial firms. It includes fields of research interest and names of research and development executives. There are both subject and geographical indexes. Those with a science or technical background will particularly find this helpful for names of potential employers.

*Lewis, M. (Ed.) *The Foundation Directory.* New York: Columbia University Press, 1971.

Directory of non-governmental, non-profit organizations established to maintain or aid social, educational, charitable, religious or other activities serving the common welfare. The two criteria for inclusion in the directory are: 1) awarded grants of $25,000 or more in that year, 2) total assets of $500,000 or more. This directory is useful in investigating foundations as potential employers, and also for preparation of proposals for grants to determine possible support. It is indexed alphabetically by state and by fields of interests.

**MacMillan Job Guide to American Corporations.* New York: MacMillan, 1967.
The guide offers a broad look at major American corporations—their goals, personnel requirements, and opportunities. Four areas covered in the guide include:

- –Description of corporations and job opportunities (This includes information on annual sales, employees, mission and products, facilities, degree requirements and opportunities and benefits.)
- –Alphabetical index to corporations
- –Index to corporations by college degrees
- –Geographical index to home offices

This book is a good place to start to find out what companies are seeking persons with a particular type of college background.

*Pingree, E. (Ed.) *Business Periodicals Index.* New York: The H.W. Wilson Co., 1971.
Indexes approximately 250-300 journals covering a wide range of industries. Excellent general reference for researching a company or an industry. It is indexed alphabetically by company and by industry, and it lists all articles within a given year relating to a particular company or industry. The index is also useful for identifying trade journals for a given field.

**Research Centers Directory.* (3rd edition) Detroit: Gale Research Co., 1968.
A directory of approximately 4,500 research institutes, centers, foundations, laboratories, bureaus and other non-profit research facilities in the U.S. and Canada. It is arranged by type of research done. Excellent for identifying research organizations in any field (social science, education, biological science, physical science, business and industrial relations, etc.). Information includes scope of research activities and names of publications, sources of funding and names and addresses of principal researchers. This directory would be helpful to those wanting to work in a particular research area or for identifying names of people who could be helpful in a job search.

**Thomas Register of American Manufacturers.* New York, New York: Thomas Publishing Co., 1971.
These eleven volumes contain detailed information on leading manufacturers throughout the country. Included in the volumes are:

Vols. 1–6	Products and services listed alphabetically
Vol. 7	Company names, addresses and telephone numbers with Capital ratings, names of company officials and locations of branch offices.
Vol. 8	Brand names
Vol. 9–11	Catalogs of companies appearing alphabetically and cross-indexed in first 8 volumes.

*Wasserman, Paul, and Greer, W.R., Jr. *Consultants and Consulting Organizations.* New York: Graduate School of Business and Public Administration, Cornell University, 1966.
This is a detailed listing of consulting firms arranged alphabetically and cross-referenced by subject field and geographical location. This could be helpful in a job search in locating companies doing independent consulting in your area of expertise. They could be considered potential employers, or persons who could describe the feasibility of starting your own consulting firm.

**West Coast Theatrical Dictionary.* Los Angeles: Tarcher/Gousha Guides, 1971.
Contains information on companies related to the entertainment industry in Los Angeles, San Francisco, Nevada, and Hawaii. There are also alphabetical listings for Chicago, Nashville, and New York. The main sections of the directory include: artists representatives, broadcasting/radio and

television and associated services, live show production, and distribution motion picture and TV production equipment, facilities and services, music, recording, tape and associated services, public relations/advertising, graphics and associated services, publishing and associated services, theatrical instruction, and unions, guilds and trade associations. For those interested in the entertainment industry this is a good source.

Women

Fairbank, Jane D. and Bryson, Helen L. *Second Careers for Women.* Second Careers for Women: Stanford, California, 1975. $4.95.

This book is written for women in the San Francisco Bay area, but much of the information is applicable to a wider audience. The Second Careers series gives descriptive information about a wide range of career fields and their applicability as a second career for women.

Friedman, Sande and Schwartz, Lois. *No Experience Necessary: A Guide to Employment for the Female Liberal Arts Graduate.* New York: Dell Publishing Co., Inc., 1971. $1.25.

An excellent guide for the female college graduate who is uncertain about what she can or wants to do in the work world. The biggest portion of the book consists of 14 chapters describing career fields that are most accessible to females with liberal arts degrees. Fields include: advertising, the art world, banking and finance, book publishing, government, magazine and newspaper publishing, nonprofit, personnel and training, public relations, television, radio, and travel. Each chapter includes a general description of the field and notes several illustrative positions. Information is also given on which beginning positions are most likely available, advancement possibilities, and salary ranges. Each chapter lists specific sources of further information. Job hunting techniques and part-time employment possibilities are both given some attention.

Higginson, Margaret and Quick, Thomas L. *The Ambitious Woman's Guide to a Successful Career.* New York: Amacom, 1975.

A book for the woman who believes her place is not in the home but up the career ladder. Specific hints and information on how to be a success in the corporate world.

Place, Irene and Armstrong, Alice. *Management Careers for Women.* Louisville, Kentucky: Vocational Guidance Manuals, Inc., 1975. $3.95 pb.

The authors have tried to combine a little of everything a woman needs to know to consider being a manager in today's economy and society. This ranges from brief descriptions of management theories to common stereotypes of women in management to a self-analysis rating. For those women just considering a management career, this might be a starter book.

Planning for Work. Catalyst: New York

One of a series of booklets written by Catalyst, "the national nonprofit organization dedicated to expanding employment opportunities for college-educated women who wish to combine career and family responsibilities." Written in a self-guidance workbook format.

Scofield, Nanette E. and Klarman, Betty. *So You Want to Go Back to Work!* New York: Random House, 1968.

A good general guide for the mature woman considering work options. The book starts by discussing the question common to women contemplating going back to work, viz., can I manage the house and care for the family's needs? The next section of the book asks readers to analyze their own situation and assess their strengths and weaknesses and outlines a number of ways to make a tentative career plan. Next, the most common career fields are described and ways to get further information are suggested.

The main portion of the book deals with the options open to the mature woman. Chapters are included on: returning to school, getting a full-time job, starting a business at home, getting a part-time job, and volunteering. Each of these options is carefully considered and examined from the perspective of the problems that would be encountered by the middle-age wife/mother. For example, in discussing the option of returning to school, consideration is given to various types of school programs including continuing education, adult education, extension program and home study. The implications of the effects of each alternative regarding home responsibilities are examined.

A planning approach is emphasized throughout the book. Women are encouraged to determine their goals, obtain the necessary information, anticipate the results of their actions, and make alternative plans to meet both their needs and the needs of the family.

Splaver, Sarah, *Nontraditional Careers for Women*. New York: Julian Messner, 1973.
A brief, but effective, overview of 500 occupations which women may consider. The book's readability is enhanced by brief success stories of women in nontraditional fields.

The New Woman's Survival Sourcebook. New York: Alfred A. Knopf, 1975.
This 245-page guidebook describes and lists resources for many concerns of today's women, including work, money, health, children, sports, education, legal issues, literature, the arts, and religion and spirituality.

Acknowledgments

The suggestions and critical reactions of David Drummond and Carol Hendrix were helpful in developing many of the ideas contained in this program. Some of the materials contained in sections V and VI were adopted from original drafts by David Drummond and Carol Hendrix respectively.

We also want to express our appreciation to Suzi Prichard and Diane Waxler. Their comments and suggestions were as valuable as their typing skill.